HAUNTED GRAVEYARDS OF THE OZARKS

DAVID E. HARKINS

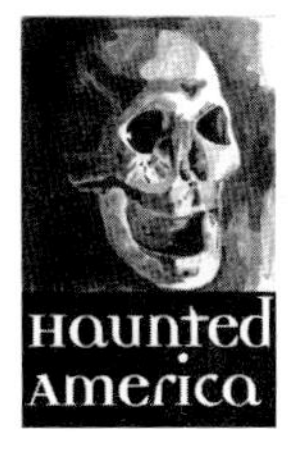

Published by Haunted America
A Division of The History Press
Charleston, SC 29403
www.historypress.net

Cover photography courtesy of Shane Wade Corkren.

All photographs by the author unless otherwise noted.

First published 2013

Manufactured in the United States

ISBN 978.1.60949.984.6

Library of Congress CIP data applied for.

Notice: The information in this book is true and complete to the best of our knowledge. It is offered without guarantee on the part of the author or The History Press. The author and The History Press disclaim all liability in connection with the use of this book.

Spirits of the Dead

Thy soul shall find itself alone
'Mid dark thoughts of the grey tomb-stone;
Not one, of all the crowd, to pry
Into thine hour of secrecy.
Be silent in that solitude,
Which is not loneliness—for then
The spirits of the dead, who stood
In life before thee, are again
In death around thee, and their will
Shall overshadow thee; be still.
The night, though clear, shall frown,
And the stars shall not look down
From their high thrones in the Heaven
With light like hope to mortals given,
But their red orbs, without beam,
To thy weariness shall seem
As a burning and a fever
Which would cling to thee forever.
Now are thoughts thou shalt not banish,
Now are visions ne'er to vanish;
From thy spirit shall they pass
No more, like dew-drop from the grass.
The breeze, the breath of God, is still,
And the mist upon the hill
Shadowy, shadowy, yet unbroken,
Is a symbol and a token.
How it hangs upon the trees,
A mystery of mysteries!

—Edgar Allan Poe, 1827

CONTENTS

Dedication and Acknowledgements

I would like to dedicate this book to my father, Edward Eugene Harkins, who passed from this life much too soon; my mother, Phyllis Harkins; and my two sisters, Lori and Robie Harkins; and a special thanks to my partner, Don Fohn, who has been my source of strength for the past thirty years. I would also like to acknowledge my fellow Ozarks Paranormal Society teammates, Shane Wade Corkren, Tonya Mulitalo, Debra Stanton, Jimmy Robison and mostly to my great friend Bud Steed, who inspired me to pursue the task of writing this book. Thanks, Bud, for your guidance and insight during this process. I would also like to thank the people of the Ozarks for inviting me into their homes and businesses and sharing their stories of history, folklore and the paranormal, which were the inspiration for writing this book.

INTRODUCTION

As gray and marbled tombstones weather and fade into the ground on the remains of those over whom they kept vigil so well, many of the departed who once called the Ozark Mountains home may very well still be with us. The Ozark Mountains have long been the source of many tales of forgotten as well as legendary characters and the mysteries that surround these "quiet cities" of wood and stone that house their earthly remains. While the names on many of the markers may have very well faded away from memory, some of these departed souls still linger within the confines of what once was. And for the living, many a ghostly tale has been passed down throughout the generations by folks living in the Ozarks.

Whether passed down by locals or the occasional passerby, these hauntings have been attributed to many factors, including grave robbery, occult rituals, unmarked and forgotten burials or natural disasters that have disturbed the resting places; many in the Ozarks believe that these occurrences may even be due to improper burials. No one really knows for sure the reason why these departed individuals still embrace this realm. Added to that, cemeteries have always held a certain mystique about them. Whether in broad daylight or on the darkest night, many of these Ozarks cemeteries have a somber feeling about them. From the more known urban necropolises to the long-forgotten family plots situated down rugged and winding gravel roads, these quiet cities of the Ozarks have the power to send chills up and down the spines of even the most hardened skeptic.

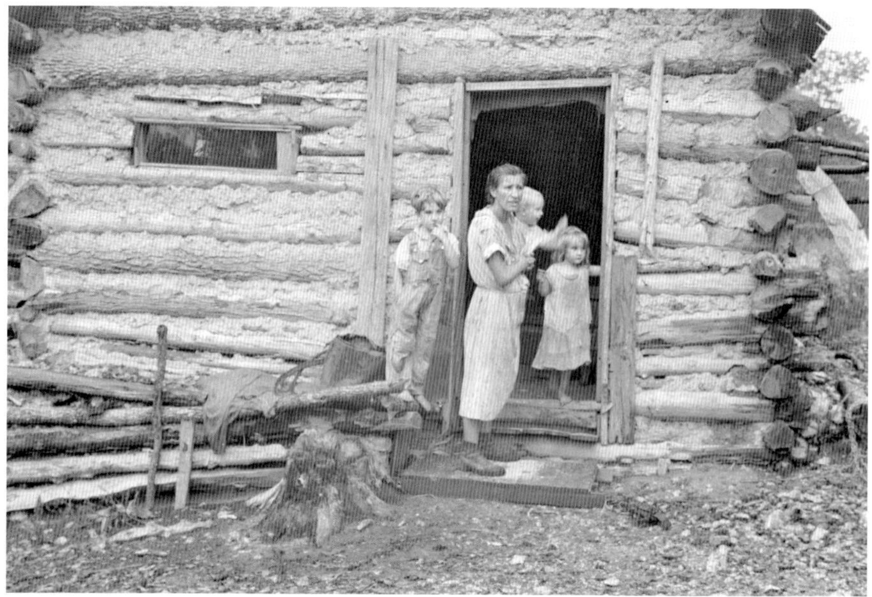

Typical Ozarks family from the early 1900s. *Courtesy of the Library of Congress.*

Along with the many tales and legends passed down through the years, numerous accounts of paranormal phenomena have been reported and experienced in the cemeteries of the Ozarks. Among them are sightings of phantom funeral processions, mysterious orbs of light, disembodied voices and even ghostly apparitions and black shadows moving about. Be it the Wilson Cemetery, which lies in a long-forgotten place in the woods that once thrived with life and wealth; Greenbrier Cemetery with its tales of ghostly apparitions of fallen Civil War soldiers; or even sightings of the apparition of mass murderer William "Cockeyed" Cook at the Peace Church Cemetery in Joplin, Missouri, tales of ghostly activity abound in these ancient Ozark hills. I invite you to follow me as I explore some of the more interesting historical accounts, legends and lore associated with the people, cemeteries and burial sites of the Ozark Mountains. Put your thoughts and judgments on the line and decide if you believe.

A Brief History of the Ozarks

The Ozarks has been home to a wide variety of peoples for thousands of years. Flint work, dating back ten thousand years or more, was left by hunters and gatherers who migrated through the region. Arrowheads, spear points and knives, which belonged to ancient Indian tribes, have been found dating back one thousand to three thousand years.

Prior to the 1800s, the Ozarks' countryside was a rugged wilderness that contained an abundance of wildlife. Since there were no roads, the White River in northwestern Arkansas became the highway of commerce for French explorers and trappers. It was the French who gave the Ozarks its name. It began as *aux arc*, which were the French words for the bows and bends in the area's streams. French Canadian trappers also made bows out of the Osage orange trees that grew in this area.

In the early 1800s, Napoleon Bonaparte, the ruler of France, was badly in need of money to finance his wars in Europe. United States president Thomas Jefferson purchased the Louisiana Territory from France in 1803. The northern part of the territory was called Upper Louisiana and included the present state of Missouri. Upper Louisiana extended northward from the thirty-third parallel to Canada and westward to the Rocky Mountains. The Ozark Mountain range extends from the southern part of Illinois, across Missouri and into Arkansas and Oklahoma.

The Ozarks Plateau rises from 1,500 to 2,300 feet above sea level, with the highest peaks being the Boston Mountains of Arkansas. The Ozarks region has a total area of about forty thousand square miles and is surrounded

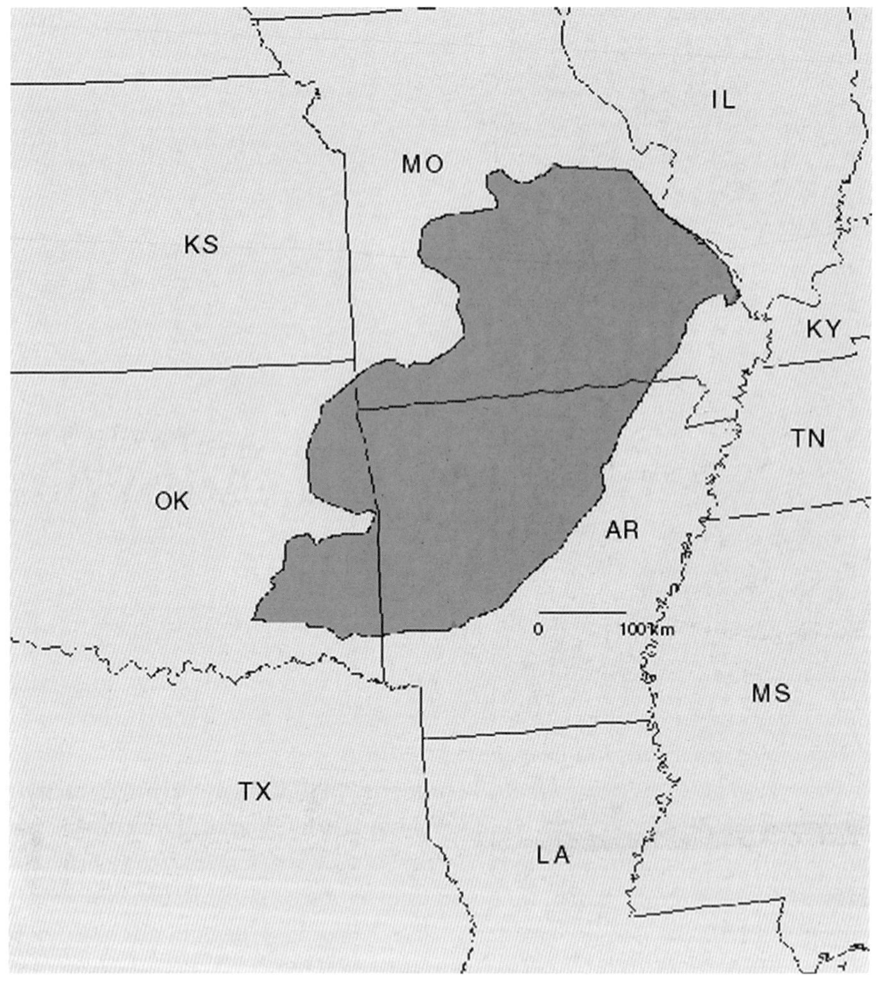

Map of the Ozark Plateau. *Courtesy of the Library of Congress.*

by the Missouri River on the north, the Mississippi River on the east, the Neosho River in Oklahoma on the west and the Boston Mountains in Arkansas on the south. The hills are covered with timber and contain rich mineral deposits.

The Osage were the last Indian tribe to live in this area. They were moved to the Indian Territories of Oklahoma in the early 1880s. During this same era, the Ozark Mountains became home to a rugged group of people of Scottish-Irish-English descent. The first white settlers to the Ozarks' hills

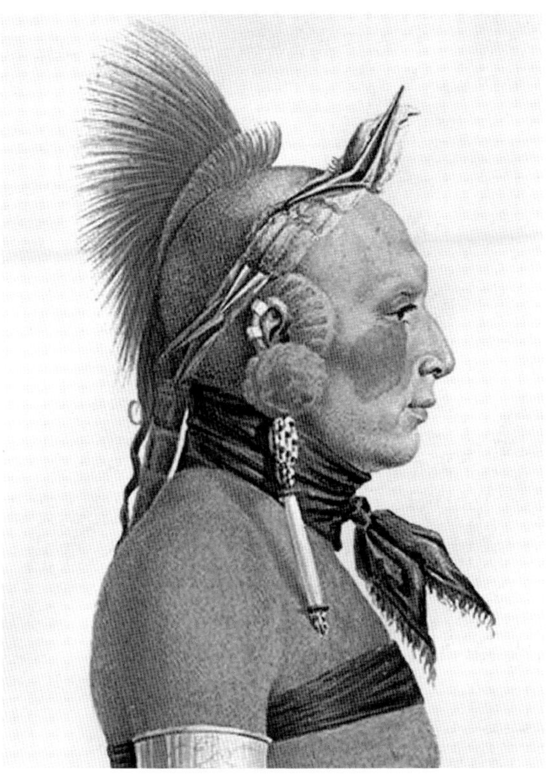

Left: An Osage Indian. *Courtesy of the Library of Congress.*

Below: An artist's rendition of an Ozarks family homestead.

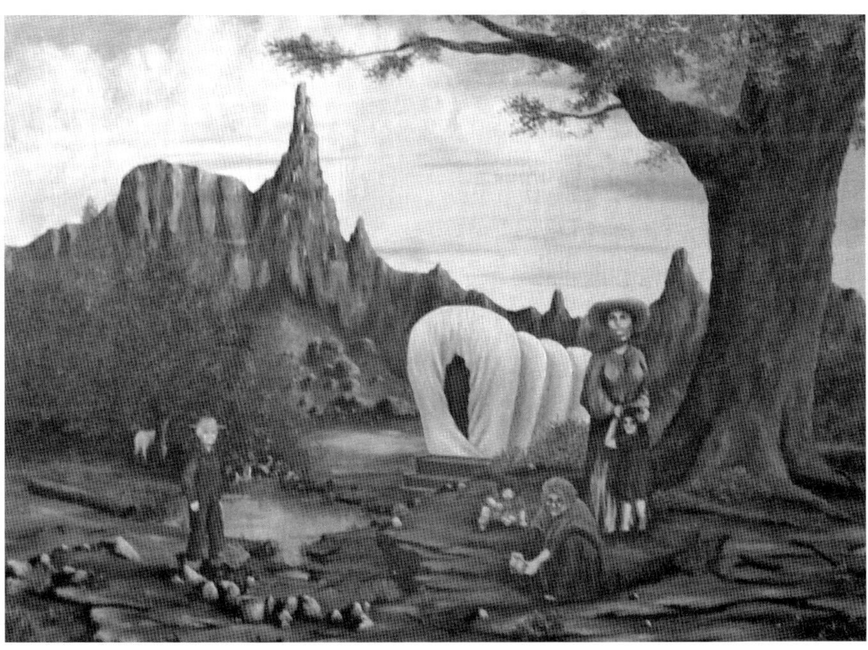

made their way up the White River in 1810. The settlers, bringing skills from the Tennessee woods, adapted well to the rugged terrain in the White River area of the Ozark Mountains. These early homesteaders kept busy building log homes, hunting, farming and rearing families. These folks migrated into this area bringing their own special culture. The Ozarks' "hillbilly" persona has cultural roots that date back several hundred years to the old country and is still prevalent in many areas of the Ozarks today. Despite the lack of scholarly consensus on the origin of the term, historian Anthony Harkins gives as the most likely explanation that Scottish highlanders melded "hill-folk" with "Billie," a word meaning friend or companion. There is no shortage of hillbilly images in American popular culture. Whether it is a barefoot, rifle-toting, moonshine-swigging, bearded man staring out from beneath a floppy felt hat or a toothless granny sitting at a spinning wheel and peering suspiciously at strangers from the front porch of a dilapidated mountain cabin, the hillbilly, in all its manifestations, is instantly recognizable. Wrapped up with the condescension in people's common view of the hillbilly is a trace of admiration for what they perceive as his independent spirit and his disregard for the trappings of modern society.

In modern American popular culture, the term hillbilly is often used interchangeably with other epithets for poor white people such as "redneck," "cracker" or "white trash." But throughout much of the twentieth century, the word hillbilly conjured a character whose geographic origins were more narrowly defined, referring to poor, uneducated whites, generally in the Appalachians or the Ozarks but not always confined to these two southern highland regions. The term "hillbilly" made its literary debut only in 1900, in the pages of the *New York Journal*, but the term was likely in common use in the rural South by the late nineteenth century. Although the subjects of the *Journal* piece were residents of the Alabama hills, the first scholarly use of the term appeared four years later in a study of Arkansas Ozarks dialect. One can argue that "hillbilly" and the Ozarks have been synonymous ever since.

Funeral Customs and Superstitions of the Ozark Mountains

Settlers to the Ozark Mountains brought burial traditions with them from their home states of Tennessee, Illinois, Alabama, Mississippi and Kentucky. Prior to the establishment of a funeral industry with undertakers, embalmers and factory-made caskets, every job associated with burial was handled by members of the deceased's community. This work required practical know-how, physical strength and access to materials and was influenced by religious custom, folklore and superstition.

The modern funerary industry evolved from the trade of cabinetmaking, when stores that made and sold furniture added wooden coffins and caskets to their wares. By the late 1800s, many such businesses also offered the use of elaborate horse-drawn hearses, burial goods (such as shrouds) and, later, embalming. The Arkansas Undertakers Association formed in 1890 but lasted only a few years, followed in 1900 by the permanent establishment of the Arkansas Funeral Directors Association. State law established a board of embalmers in 1909.

Embalming was slow to gain acceptance, especially in rural communities where it was deemed unnecessary, as burial routinely took place within twenty-four hours of death. African Americans, however, traditionally delayed burial for as much as a week. This was done in order to hold the funeral on a Sunday. This custom originated during the days of slavery when Sunday was the only day slaves were given time to bury their dead.

Death almost always took place nearby or in the home. Family members nursed their patient by day, but as death approached, neighbors would begin

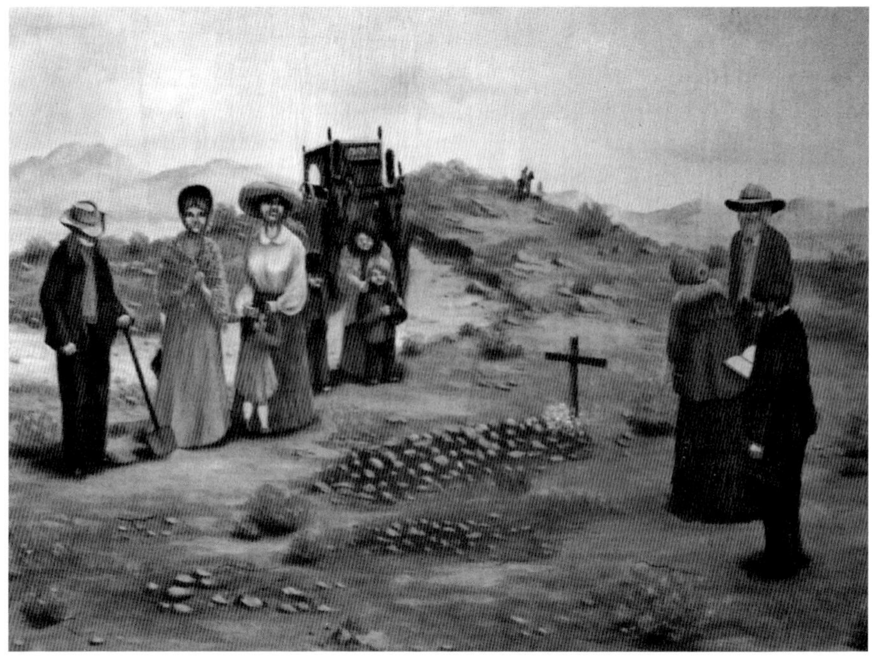

An artist's rendition of an Ozarks funeral from the 1800s.

the practice of "sitting up" each night. In addition to providing nursing, those who sat up ensured that the dying person did not die alone and that the family members would be awakened to be present at the passing of their loved one. As soon as a death occurred, members of the community would undertake many tasks required for the burial of the departed. Family members did not participate in the preparation of the body, except when the loved one's death resulted from a highly contagious disease, such as diphtheria, cholera or smallpox, in which case fear of contamination would most surely keep members of the community away.

The first order of business was to lay out the deceased's body before rigor mortis (the stiffening of the deceased's muscles) began to set in. This entailed placing the deceased in a supine position on a flat surface, where it would be bathed and dressed in new or clean clothing and coins placed over the eyes to keep them shut; if the eyes are found open, it is thought to be a bad omen. Coins were chosen for two reasons. They prevented the staring of the corpse, as it was believed that the dead person was looking for someone to accompany him and you didn't want him casting an eye on you. The coins were heavy enough to weigh the lids down. The second reason was the long-held belief that a corpse needed money to pay its way into the next world. Then a cloth was tied around the jaw to keep it from flopping open and the arms were folded across the chest. Another towel, soaked in a strong soda solution, took care of discoloration. Spices or cedar chips placed around the body helped ward off any unpleasant odors, especially in summer.

The practice of embalming was not widely practiced before the Civil War, but the necessity of shipping battle dead long distances called for a cheap way to preserve the body during transit. Formaldehyde became the elixir of choice. After the Civil War, funeral parlors began using the techniques learned during the war to preserve corpses, but in the Ozarks, undertakers were few and far between and the lack of embalming caused some unpleasant situations.

There are many accounts of a body suddenly sitting up in the middle of the funeral service. The cause of this horrible sight was rigor mortis. One account tells of a stubborn corpse suddenly rising in its coffin. The funeral was halted while some of the men in the congregation strained and sweated to get the body back into a supine position. When they got his back down, his legs rose up. When they got his legs down, the rest of him rose up. Finally, the lid was nailed down on the coffin and the service pressed on to a hasty conclusion.

While the body was still in the house, certain precautions were taken to ensure the welfare of the living. For instance, the body was always laid out on the first floor of the house, never on the second. If a step squeaked while the body was still under the roof, there would be a death in the family within a year. All cats would have to be locked up in a different room to prevent them from leaping over the corpse. Such an act was considered the easiest way to have bad luck enter the house, and the cat would have to be killed immediately. It was believed that if a cat that had leaped over the corpse were allowed to live, the first living person it would leap toward would go blind. Other friends and neighbors would bring food to the deceased's home, scrub the deceased's room and bedstead and do laundry. And, most importantly, superstition required that when death finally occurred, one of the bereaved neighbors should rise immediately from the bedside and stop all the clocks in the household. Everybody knows that if a clock should happen to stop by itself while a corpse is lying in the house, another member of the family would die within a year, and it was considered best to take no chances in such matters.

The next thing to be done was to cover every mirror in the house with white cloths, which were not to be removed until after the funeral. This was done out of consideration for those who may come to view the body, for if one of them should glimpse their own reflection in the deceased's house, it was believed that they would never live to see another summer. It was also believed that covering up the mirror would prevent the deceased's soul from being caught and trapped in the mirror. After death, all the windows and doors in the house would be opened in order that the soul of the dead would be released and fly away.

In the meantime, a local carpenter, or often the town's blacksmith, would build either a coffin or casket. Coffins, the older of the two styles, were hexagonal boxes tapered at the feet, with a separate, one-piece lid. The rectangular casket, a style used today, has a two-part lid attached to one side of the box with a hinge, which permits the body to be viewed from the waist up.

Although some of the larger towns had stores that sold coffins and caskets, time was of the essence, and most people preferred to have the box built locally whenever possible. As these were almost never made in advance of death, builders usually had to work through the night to complete one for burial the following day. Meanwhile, the body, lying on boards and covered with a sheet, was never left unattended; neighbors sat up with the corpse all night for as long as it remained unburied. The primary reason for doing this was the belief that the soul remained with the body for twenty-four hours after death, and this practice kept the soul company and prevented it from being whisked away by the devil. Others felt that it was necessary to keep cats or other vermin from disfiguring the corpse.

Prior to the advent of telephones, and in towns having only weekly newspapers, notifying the public of the death and the time and place of the funeral was done by word of mouth: tolling a church or school bell (usually one ring for each year that the deceased had lived) or handing out small funeral notices. The obituary would be published at a later date and often contained such information as the cause of death, the deceased's virtues and dying words and a sentimental poem.

Once the coffin was delivered and the body placed within, a funeral would be held most typically in the home, at a church or school or in the cemetery. In the era of the circuit-riding minister (used by most denominations), the funeral service might be delayed until the minister made his next visit, often from a few weeks to several months later. The coffined body would be conveyed to the cemetery in a wagon (later in a pickup truck or hearse). It was considered to be bad luck if the funeral procession was forced to stop en route. This is the origin of the modern custom of cars pulling to one side of the road when meeting a funeral procession, now deemed an act of respect.

Another custom required that the grave be dug on the day of the burial; digging in advance was believed to invite other deaths within the family or the community. If this digging had to be done earlier, a token amount of loose dirt would be left in the bottom and removed on the day of the burial, thereby finishing the grave on the proper day. If a person died at night or early in the morning, the grave was dug after noon on the following day. It was also considered bad luck to be buried to the north side of a church. This belief arose out of the days when criminals, stillborn babies and suicides were customarily buried to the north and west sides, while the good Christians were buried to the south and east sides of the church. Over the years, people might not have known why they thought it was bad luck to be buried on the north side, not realizing that they had a deep-seated remembrance that it was only "bad and cursed" people who were buried there.

At the cemetery, the coffin's lid would be removed so that mourners could take a last look at the body before the lid was nailed on. The box would then be lowered into the grave using ropes or harness reins. One never left in the middle of a burial, as it was bad luck to leave before the grave was filled in.

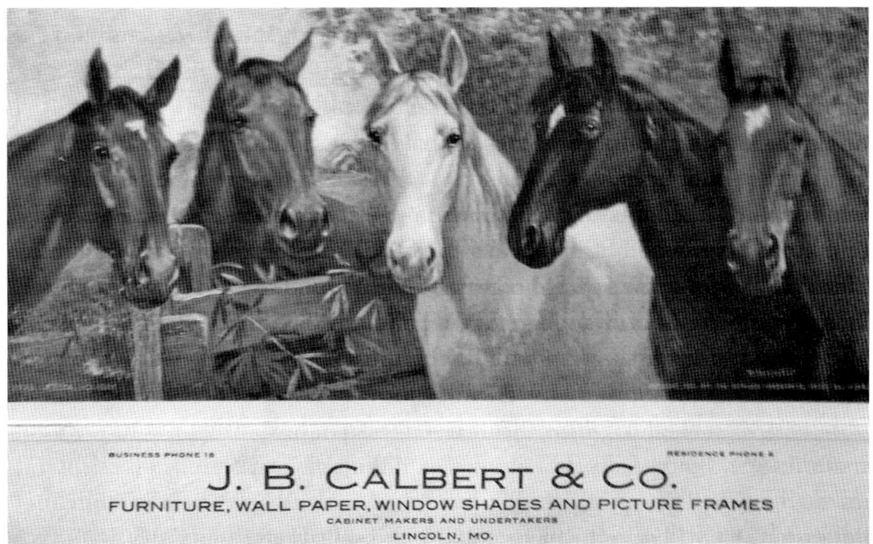

An old advertisement for a furniture maker and undertaker in Lincoln, Missouri, 1913.

After the burial of her husband, a grieving widow was expected to enter a period of mourning. She would wear nothing but the traditional black mourning garb, and she would give away all her colored clothing because that was considered good luck. Once this was done, the widow then labored under a whole bevy of restrictions. She could not court again until a full year after the death of her husband and not marry for two years after that. The widow was required to visit the grave of her late husband at least four times a week during mourning. She could not speak to another man, unless it was a member of her family or the preacher, until the grave was filled. She could not sing any song unless it was a church hymn, and she could not participate in any kind of social activities except for attending church functions. She was forbidden to eat any sort of sweets or drink any type of liquor or any sweet drink except coffee. Nor was she allowed to smoke, chew tobacco or take snuff. If a widow mourned for more than one year, it was also considered bad luck. With restrictions like that hanging over her head, I would dare say that one year of serious lament was more than sufficient.

Decoration Day, following a cemetery cleanup day, was a much-anticipated event that combined family reunions, speeches, prayers and music, a communal dinner and the decorating of graves. The custom is no longer the major event that it once was, but it is still observed in some cemeteries across the Ozarks.

Labor-intensive burial customs performed by local citizens gradually died out, beginning in the larger cities, as undertakers assumed all the jobs once performed by neighbors. In rural communities, these customs lasted far longer but had mostly ended by the 1950s since most funeral homes sold burial insurance policies, thus easing the transition from the home funeral to ones managed by the commercial funeral industry.

With all these superstitions and customs being so widely believed and seared into the minds of the folks who inhabited the Ozarks in the old days, could it be possible that they took these beliefs to the grave with them and what we experience today as "ghosts" and paranormal activity may be a result of these superstitions being violated or not upheld?

Part I

Missouri Ozarks

Then away, out in the woods I heard that kind of a sound that a ghost makes when it wants to tell about something that's on its mind and can't make itself understood, and so can't rest easy in its grave, and has to go about that way every night grieving.

—*Mark Twain,* The Adventures of Huckleberry Finn

The Witches Foundation

LEBANON

Having lived near Lebanon, Missouri, since 1985, I have heard almost every version of the legends of the "Foundation of Death" or the "Witches Foundation," as the locals call it. The Witches Foundation is an old house place and cemetery located outside Lebanon, near what was once called the Old Wire Road during the Civil War due to the telegraph lines that once ran down it. Originally there was an old house situated in the middle of the small graveyard, but many years ago it burned down. After the fire, the present owners discovered five graves in the formation of a pentagram within the confines of the foundation, hence the name "Witches Foundation." Just outside the foundation are many other graves that, oddly, face every direction except for the traditional Christian practice of facing the graves toward the east. The city has no history of the cemetery except for it being listed as a family plot. Other than that, it is unknown who founded the graveyard and why the graves face every direction possible. An even stranger question remains as to why the five graves are situated inside the old foundation. Local legend has it that the graveyard is a burial site for witches who once lived on the outskirts of town. Although this is just local speculation and not based on any facts, I have to chalk it up to being a rural legend. Over the years, the foundation has been a popular party spot for local teenagers, and as a result, many of the graves have been vandalized and many of the tombstones have been stolen.

Along with the speculation of this being a burial site for witches, many stories of paranormal activity have been reported over the years. I have

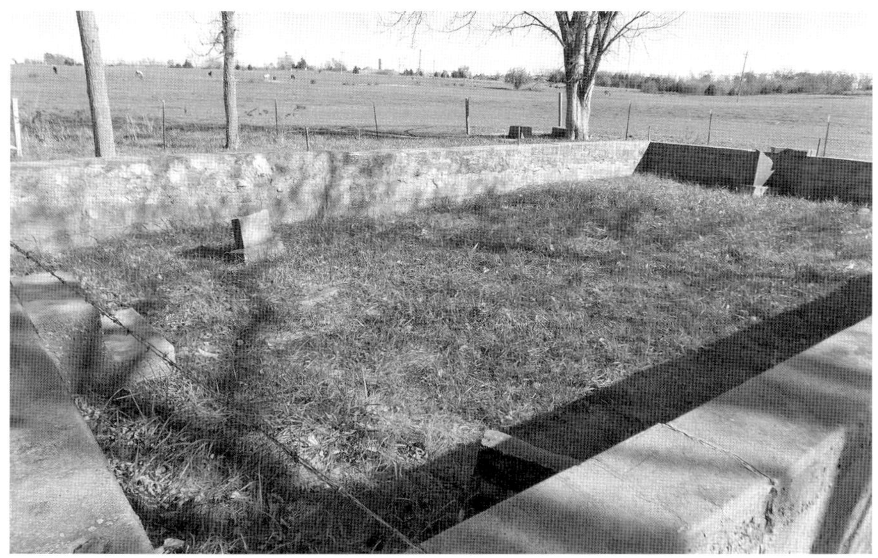

The graves inside the Witches Foundation, Lebanon, Missouri.

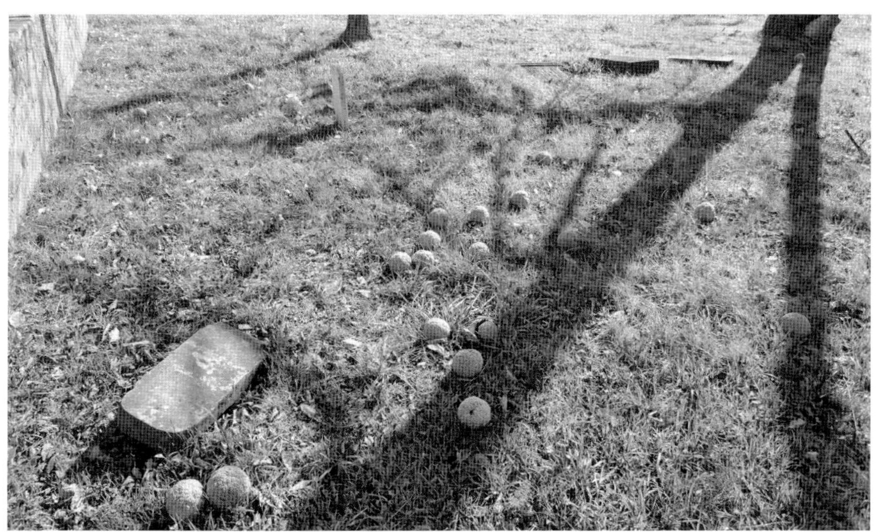

Scattered graves outside the Witches Foundation.

heard numerous tales of paranormal activity, but they mostly consist of high school kids going there to drink beer and play with Ouija boards. Some others claim that when you go to leave, your vehicle won't start, and once you finally get it started a glowing ball of light will chase you down the road for a mile or so. Others tell of a strange fog-like mist that only appears inside the graveyard, and a cloaked black figure is also often sighted. I'm not sure how many of these tales are true, as I have never experienced anything out of the ordinary there myself. If you decide to venture to the old foundation without permission, remember, the police have started regularly patrolling it, and the owners do have the right to shoot trespassers, so explore with extreme caution and respect for both the living and the dead.

CHURCH OF GOD FAITH OF ABRAHAM CEMETERY

MORSE MILL

Church of God Faith of Abraham Cemetery, also known as "Soul Keepers Cemetery," located in Morse Mill, Missouri, has had its share of reported hauntings over the years. People have reported hearing voices when no one is speaking, being touched and even seeing what appears to be an apparition lurching out from behind trees and tombstones. On the surface this seems to be just another well-kept cemetery here in the beautiful Ozarks hills, but can it be that something more sinister is at play? Some of the local residents and visitors to this "quiet city" attribute at least some of the paranormal activity to the fact that one of America's most prolific and possibly the first reported female serial killer is interred here, as well as at least seven of her victims.

Bertha Gifford was born in 1876 near the town of Morse Mill, Missouri, about six miles from Hillsboro in a beautiful section of Jefferson County. She was one of four children in a family considered one of the area's finest and most respectable. Her family worshiped in the Church of God (Faith of Abraham), a fundamentalist church that holds that the "Kingdom of God will be established on earth when Christ returns personally and visibly to reign as King in Jerusalem." It is not a pulpit-thumping, revival-sweating church; it's a dignified sect, and its members study the Bible with quiet intensity. They are sometimes mockingly called "soul sleepers" because of their literal interpretation of the prophesied resurrection, their belief that all the earth's dead lie waiting in their graves for a single day of judgment.

In her early twenties, Bertha married a man named Henry Graham. They operated the Morse Mill Hotel for a time and also farmed. The Morse Mill Hotel still stands today and has a long history as a private residence, hotel, speakeasy, brothel, halfway house, Confederate field hospital, Underground Railroad stop, Indian burial site, post office and scene of multiple murders and hangings spanning decades. In addition, several known outlaws, gangsters and murderers have visited and stayed here. It is known today to be one of the most paranormally active sites in the Midwest.

Several years after marrying Henry, seemingly out of the blue, Bertha took up with a single man who was seven years younger than her, which was quite the scandal among the townsfolk. Henry, too, was said to be keeping company with a "friend," and the marriage became bitter and mean and was marked by constant quarrels.

The "other" man in Bertha's life was Gene Gifford, a good-looking and affable carpenter and farmer. One of the larger houses he built in Morse Mill still stands, and he helped design and construct the first permanent building for the Church of God, of which he, too, was a member. It was a graceful white country church with a delicate, needle-like steeple.

Gene was a popular man around the region, a good worker, fine storyteller and good friend to all. But people said that he changed some after taking up with Bertha. His life certainly did. At the time he hooked up with Bertha, he was engaged to be married to another woman but quickly broke that off. Folks around Morse Mill muttered that Bertha, now in her early thirties and still one of the most beautiful women in town, was exerting a strange influence over Gene.

Not long after Gene and Bertha began spending time together, Bertha's husband, Henry, came down with what was diagnosed as pneumonia. He held on for a while and even rallied, with Bertha in constant attendance at his bedside. But the disease weakened him, and he developed complications including violent, agonizing stomach cramps. Henry was thirty-four years old when he died.

Following a respectable interval, and after collecting the insurance, Bertha Graham married Gene Gifford, and they left Jefferson County, moving to Catawissa, where they took up farming. Strangely, although Gene was successful at raising cattle, hogs and corn, the Giffords never bought a place of their own. Bertha didn't want to settle permanently; she liked moving from farm to farm.

In her old farmhouse, known now as the Catawissa House of Mystery, Mrs. Bertha Gifford held herself ready to dash for the bedside of every dying

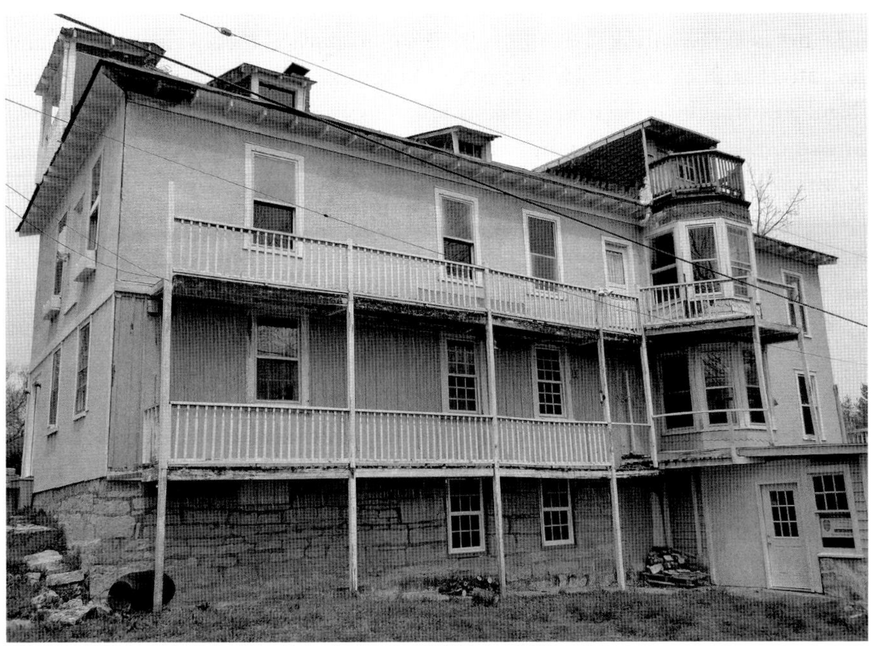

Morse Mill Hotel, Morse Mill, Missouri.

neighbor within twenty miles. Uncomplainingly, in fact eagerly, she would jump out of her warm bed in the middle of the night, put on her white nurse's uniform that was always hanging on the chair and drive her old car (or before that the horse-and-buggy) through any sort of weather. Even in blizzards, when no wheel could turn, she would plow her way on foot along cow paths between ten-foot drifts. Nothing could stop this determined woman, who usually managed to get there ahead of the country doctor.

Bertha, now fifty years old but once the belle of Meramec Valley, really was a Good Samaritan—provided her patients actually went through with the program of dying as expected. In that case, with prayers, tears and tender ministrations, she eased their last moments, and she never asked money for her services. The only trouble with Bertha, the police say, was that when her patients rallied and gave promise of recovery, she resented such attempts to cheat the grave and fed them rat poison.

Mrs. Gifford had a passion for deathbeds and funerals, of which she missed only one in eighteen years. But just as youths sometimes become so overenthusiastic about running to fires that they finally get to setting some themselves, this deathbed fan, it is charged, could not resist the temptation when anyone started to withdraw from the edge of the grave to just push him in with a little arsenic. She took command of the funerals too and liked to see everything done right, even going so far as to pay for the embalming of one of her victims.

Mrs. Gifford, though not a trained nurse, was a very competent volunteer, as local doctors well knew. She could keep temperature and nourishment charts, understood symptoms and drugs and therefore might be allowed discretion in administering medicines. Bertha seems to have preferred children for her patients whenever she could get them. The police say this was because they would trustfully swallow anything she gave them as long as it did not taste too nasty, and they never presumed to correct any misstatement she might make to the doctor. When Bertha took charge of a case she took command of the household, ordering this in and that out of the sickroom and impressing the family in countless ways with her superior knowledge and experience. Early in the evening, in her kind but firm professional manner, she would turn to the mother and say, "Now, my dear, I want you to go to bed and get a good night's rest so you can take my place tomorrow. Don't worry, I am here."

This was really a command, and a reasonable one. The mother, relieved to know that her child was in more competent hands than her own, would always obey. Thus, Mrs. Gifford had a whole night, free from witnesses, alone with the helpless child.

Shortly before the rising hour next morning, when she roused the family and telephoned for the doctor, the little patient would be too far gone to dispute the nurse's statement that the turn for the worse had just come in. And the parents would comfort themselves with the thought that their baby had had the best of care in her last hours. After the child's death, Bertha would weep harder than any of the family members.

As might be expected, it was the local women who first suspected Bertha, thinking it strange that whenever that ministering angel "plunks herself down in a sickroom, the patient never gets well." The men scoffed, but the women kept right on putting two and two together, and when Ed Brinley died, the ninth in the House of Mystery itself and the seventeenth under Bertha's care, all with the same symptoms, they demanded an investigation of this "bedside saint" who had consecrated her life to good works. The authorities took notice and questioned the impressively indignant Bertha.

Mrs. Gifford explained each one of the deaths plausibly. They were from acute gastritis caused by the rural habit of eating a heavy dinner at noon and then laboring on a full stomach instead of having the main meal at night after the day's work is over, as the city man has learned to do. The physicians must have been satisfied because they had issued death certificates. Could a lot of ignorant gossips know more than the doctors?

Dr. James Stewart, state health commissioner, must have thought they could because he had the records of drugstores in the neighboring towns examined and learned that Mrs. Gifford had been a steady customer of arsenic rat poison, which produces symptoms quite similar to gastritis. Also, she had made her purchases in some cases just before the deaths in question. Bertha, a picture of outraged innocence, was brought over before the grand jury, threatening slander suits all the while.

The chain of coincidences went back to 1909, when nobody thought it strange that Mr. Graham, the public benefactor's last husband, died of cramps in the night before the doctor arrived at his bedside at Morse Mill Hotel.

The next to succumb of "ptomaine poisoning," in 1913, was her new mother-in-law, Mrs. Emilie Gifford, in spite of Bertha's seemingly heroic efforts. Here Bertha's grief was not so great but was considered adequate for a daughter-in-law. A year later, her thirteen-year-old brother-in-law, James Gifford, passed out in Mrs. Gifford's arms with those same symptoms of stomach cramps and vomiting.

George Stuhlfelder told the grand jury how this "ministering angel," for whom he felt nothing but gratitude at the time, had nursed his three children—Bernard, fifteen months old; Margaret, two years old; and Irene, seven years old—for small ailments that promptly turned into acute gastritis and ended in the death of them all.

George L. Shamel, a hired man who had worked at the Gifford place, testified to the deaths of his two boys:

> *I worked off and on for the Gifford's about 18 years. I went to the Gifford place once in 1925, on a Saturday night. On the very next day, the Sabbath, my boy, Lloyd, nine years old, had stomach cramps. Two days later he died after being sick at his stomach all the time. The doctor said it was acute gastritis but didn't know what caused it. There was no post mortem performed. Five weeks later my other boy Elmer; he was seven years old; got sick with stomach cramps. He lived two days too. They said it was the same gastritis. There was no post mortem. I always trusted the Gifford's and thought it was just my luck when the boys died.*

Hardly a month after Elmer's funeral, Mrs. Gilford learned that Mrs. Leona Slocum, Shamel's sister, a tuberculosis sufferer, was "sinking." Bertha put on her nurse's uniform of white, rushed to the bedside and took charge.

Sure enough, Mrs. Slocum rallied so strongly that they were just telling the Good Samaritan that there was no longer any need of taking advantage of her kindness when the patient suddenly developed alarming stomach pains and nausea and died.

After that the survivors of the Shamel family, while not exactly suspicious, decided that Mrs. Gifford was unlucky. But the Stuhlfelders took a chance once more on Mrs. Mary Stuhlfelder, age seventy-four, with the invariable result: death from gastritis.

Quite similar were the last moments of James Ogle, a hired man of the Giffords who had incidentally complained that he could not collect the money they owed him. Bertha, however, paid the money in time for it to be spent on the funeral.

S. Herman Pounds, one of the strongest physical specimens in the neighborhood, indulged a bit too much in his own hard cider and went to sleep in the Gifford pasture. Bertha had him brought into the house and gave him something to sober up. "Acute gastritis, super induced by alcoholism," she told the doctor, who arrived too late.

There was the sudden onset of this same stomach trouble carrying off "Grandma" Birdie Unnerstall just as Bertha dropped in for a visit while everyone was away.

Mrs. Laura Brown, of East St. Louis, aunt of little seven-year-old Mary Brown, one of Mrs. Gifford's alleged poison victims, tells a sample of Mrs. Gifford's nursing. "One afternoon about two and a half months before Mary died," Mrs. Brown said, "she was lying ill in the bedroom. I entered. Mrs. Gifford was sitting by the bedside; she seemed annoyed by my presence. I had come all the way from East St. Louis to Catawissa to visit the sick child and mentioned that I was tired. Mrs. Gifford urged, 'Why don't you lie down and take a little nap.'"

The last of the list was Ed Brinley, a neighbor and another cider victim who rested for a fatal moment against the mailbox post outside the Gifford house. Bertha's watchful eye spotted him there, and she ordered her husband to carry him in. When, two hours later, he also had met his death from the same old symptoms, even the men admitted that it was odd.

The grand jury thought so too and indicted Bertha for murder, but she still persisted in her denials until Andrew McConnell, chief of police of Webster Groves, a suburb of St. Louis, took a hand. He noticed that the prisoner seemed especially annoyed at the suggestion that she had poisoned Beulah Mounds, the three-year-old daughter of S. Herman Pounds. He harped on that case until, according to McConnell, she

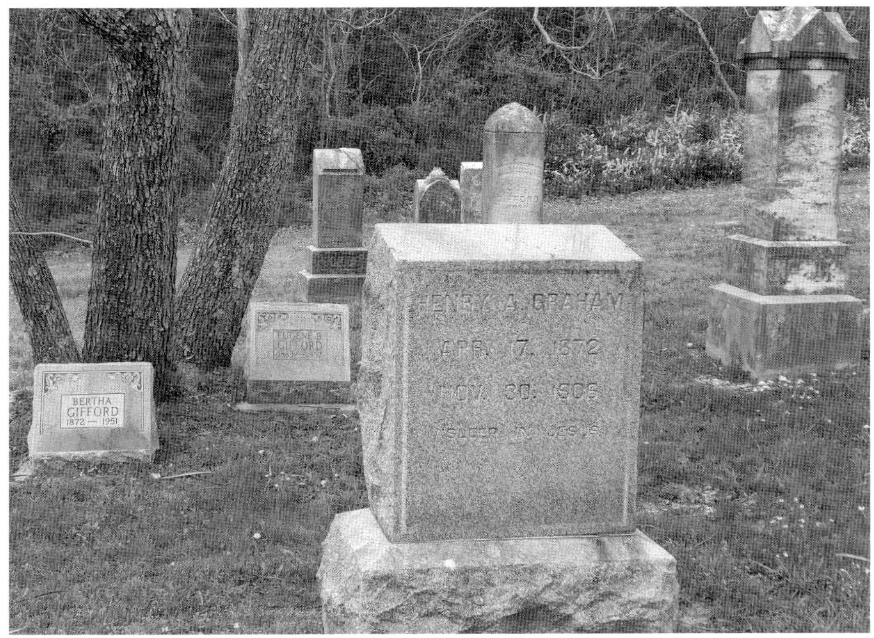

The grave of Bertha Gifford and the graves of her first and second husbands, one of whom she murdered. *Courtesy of Shane Wade Corkren.*

finally snapped at him, "Well, anyway, I did not give any arsenic to that Pounds child."

"To whom did you give it?" the chief asked quietly. Her answer, he says, was a confession that she had poisoned Brinley, the Shamel boys and perhaps some others. Her excuse was that she wanted to put them out of their misery. Brinley's body was exhumed, and its stomach showed traces of arsenical poisoning, according to the police. Since the confession, Bertha's chief ambition was to avoid being photographed. She sat in her cell with a blanket ready to throw over her head whenever she heard a footfall in the corridor. She exhibited remorse, too, and said she did not care to live.

Following the three-day trial, Bertha was found not guilty by reason of insanity and committed to the Missouri State Mental Hospital at Farmington, where she remained until her death in 1951.

Although counts vary, most historians and family members agree that Gifford actually killed at least seventeen people over a period of twenty-four years. So if you're ever in the vicinity of Morse Mill, stop on by the old cemetery or the Morse Mill Hotel and you may just catch a glimpse of Ms. Bertha or one of her many victims.

Wilson's Cemetery

Richland

For many people in the areas of Lebanon and Richland, Missouri, there is one place that is steeped in mystery and local lore that goes back for generations. Wilson's Cemetery is a small family plot located down several miles of winding gravel roads in Laclede County just off Interstate 44. For most of the year, many of its regal tombstones can barely be seen due to the overgrowth that surrounds them, and if you're not looking, you may just pass this forgotten place. Over the years, Wilson's Cemetery has been a party place for local teenagers, as evident by the amount of trash and beer bottles that litter the area just outside its fence. It is unknown who now owns the land where the cemetery sits, but it's quite clear that no one in living memory is buried there due to the age of the graves and the unkempt state that the cemetery is in.

Wilson's Cemetery is known locally for the paranormal activity that has been experienced there for many decades. Tales of apparitions and fog-like mists are commonly reported in the area, as well as many hearing the voices of the dead speaking out to them. Upon nearing the graveyard, many people report a heavy feeling of dread and sadness, a feeling of something unseen forcing them to leave the area. Many others report that upon leaving the cemetery, their vehicles fail to start, but after pushing them down the hill a ways from the cemetery they start right up.

On a recent journey to the cemetery, I had a very strange thing happen, as witnessed by two friends who accompanied me on this visit. We stopped off on the first Richland exit on I-44 to get fuel for the truck we were in

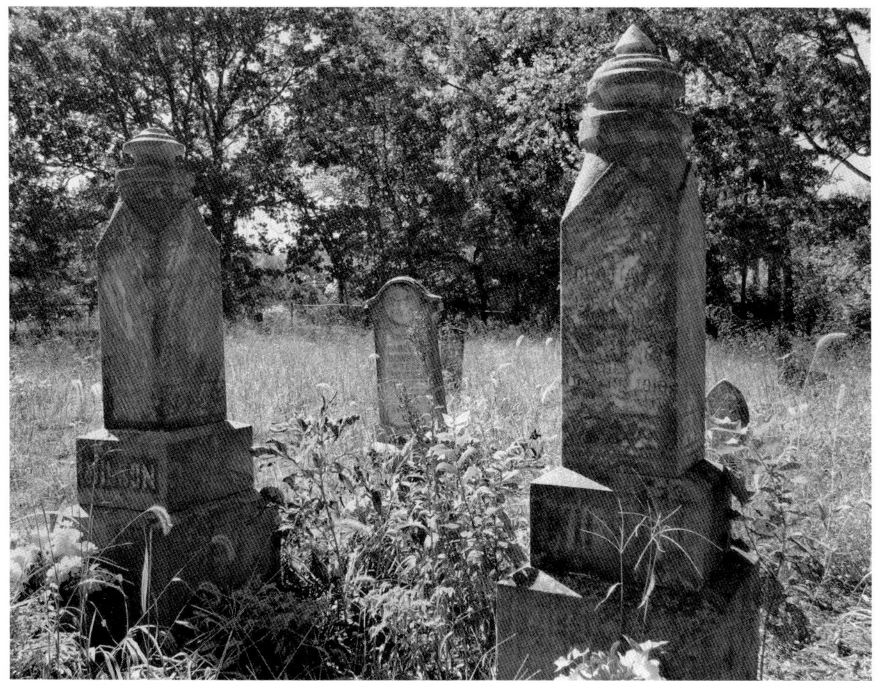

Wilson's Cemetery near Richland, Missouri.

and headed down toward Wilson's Cemetery. As we got onto the gravel road, I reset the trip counter to measure the five miles it takes to reach the cemetery. After about four miles of traveling down the old gravel road, I noticed that the trip counter had frozen up and the fuel gauge, which had just read almost full, was now down to less than an eighth of a tank of gas. In a bit of a panic, we started looking for a place to turn around to head back up to the interstate and get more fuel when all of a sudden we looked over and there was the cemetery. Being so concerned with what we had just experienced, we decided to leave the truck running as we jumped out and took a few photos.

As reported by many other folks who visit Wilson's Cemetery, the feeling of dread was upon us as we jumped back into the vehicle and headed back up the old gravel road to get fuel. A mile or so back up the road and away from Wilson's Cemetery, all the gauges in the truck started functioning normally again. Was this something paranormal in nature, or was it just some sort of electrical malfunction with the vehicle? I'm not really sure, but I know it's not happened again since that day.

Another ghostly tale of the old graveyard was recently told to me by a gentleman in his eighties who has been a grave digger in the Richland area for over sixty years. He described an odd occurrence involving Wilson's Cemetery and what is thought to be the source of one of the many hauntings there. Originally founded by brothers Mayfield and Fred Wilson, two very wealthy farmers in the area, Wilson's Cemetery had become unkempt and overgrown with weeds. With them both being up in years, the brothers found it difficult to keep the family graveyard up to the pristine shape that they once had. One day just after the War Between the States ended, a man who had been a soldier came into the area looking for work and offered to clean up the old graveyard for the two brothers. They both obliged, and the stranger spent three long days working to get the family plot back to its former glory.

After the stranger had finished cleaning up the old graveyard, the brothers went to pay the man for his days of labor when, much to their surprise, the man refused payment but instead asked that in return for his labor they grant him a burial plot in their small cemetery. The brothers both agreed to this and the man went happily on his way.

A few days later, the brothers were shocked to hear that the stranger who had been so kind to them had been killed in a freak accident working for another family in the area. As promised, the brothers had the man buried in the family cemetery, where his tomb can still be seen today. Although the inscription is unreadable due to weathering, the stone is clearly that of a soldier and is located on the left side of the cemetery where there are many children and slaves buried. Many local residents near the old cemetery believe that the spirit of the stranger is still at unrest and haunts the area to this day. What many think to be the apparition of the stranger is seen wandering the road near the cemetery quite regularly. If you ever find yourself in the vicinity of Wilson's Cemetery, make sure you have a full tank of gas and plenty of courage!

Lonesome Hill Cemetery

Phillipsburg

Located just off Interstate 44 near the small town of Phillipsburg, Missouri, is Lonesome Hill Cemetery. Lonesome Hill has become a very popular spot for local ghost hunters due to the many claims of paranormal activity that have surrounded it for decades. Local legend says there are witches buried at the back of the cemetery and one of the nearby trees was used to hang people. After visiting the cemetery, I had to laugh at the speculation that witches were buried there. After surveying the tombstones, I found that these supposed "witches' graves" were actually graves of folks who had belonged to the Order of the Eastern Star, a Freemasonry-related fraternal organization open to both men and women. Founded in 1850, the order is based on teachings from the Bible but is open to people of all religious beliefs. Members of the order must be eighteen or older; men must be Master Masons, and women must have specific relationships with Masons. Originally, a woman would have to be the daughter, widow, wife, sister or mother of a Master Mason, but the order now allows other relatives.

I suppose these rumors of witches being interred at Lonesome Hill can be attributed to the heavy influence of Fundamentalist Baptist and Pentecostal beliefs of the area and their lack of understanding of the symbology adopted by the order. The emblem of the order is a five-pointed star or inverted pentagram with the white ray of the star pointing down toward the manger. In many Christian faiths, this symbol has become synonymous with evil, as it is also used by many pagan groups as the symbol of the Baphomet, also an inverted pentagram representing a "Sabbatical Goat." It also represents

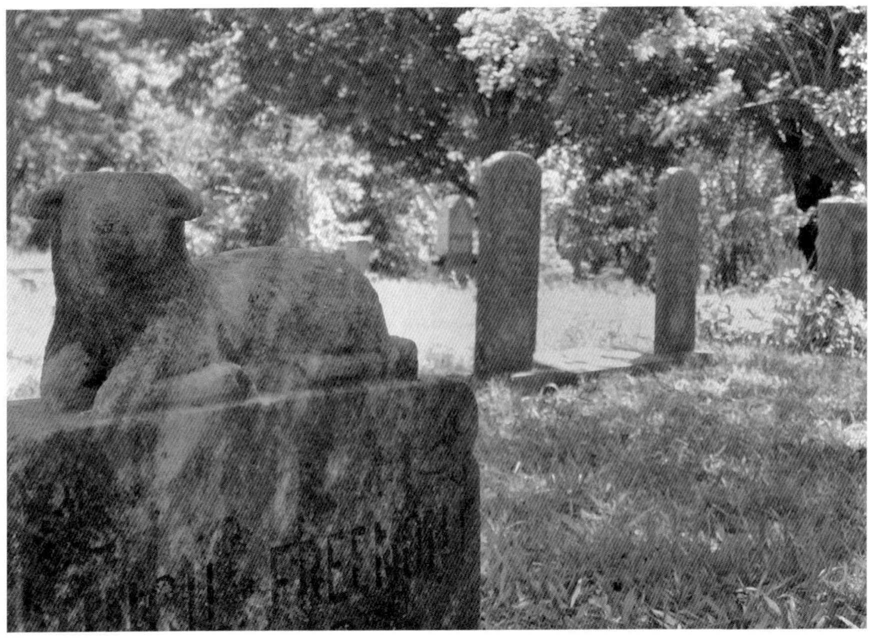

Lonesome Hill Cemetery, Phillipsburg, Missouri.

the duality of male and female, as well as Heaven and Hell or night and day, signified by the raising of one arm and the downward gesture of the other. It can be taken, in fact, to represent any of the major harmonious dichotomies of the cosmos. However, Baphomet has been connected with Satanism as well, primarily due to the adoption of its symbol by the Church of Satan. Mysteries breed suspicion.

After speaking with one of the locals who has many relatives buried at Lonesome Hill, I was informed that there once was a hanging tree very near to the cemetery, but it is now long gone. I was also told that there are many slaves buried in the cemetery in unmarked graves, but no one is really sure of the exact location of these graves, as they have fallen from memory with time. Over the years, many visitors to Lonesome Hill have reported seeing a blue mist-like form that seems to expand in size and follow you around the graveyard both during the light of day as well as in the dark nighttime hours. Many others have reported being touched or grabbed when no one else is near, and some claim to hear the voices of the dead calling out to them. In the 1980s, Lonesome Hill was a very popular party place for local teenagers. Many kids would come to party, and others would come for the thrill of possibly seeing a ghost or a chance to scare unsuspecting friends with a Ouija Board.

This once very spooky cemetery has now lost some of its mysterious charm due to a giant water tower being erected in recent years near the rear of the cemetery and the power station that now flanks the entrance with its high-tension wires running directly through the cemetery. The stories of the hauntings at Lonesome Hill are still told and retold to this day. In recent years, Lonesome Hill Cemetery has become a site of interest to many local paranormal researchers and investigators due to the legends of the hauntings that surround it.

Many believe that the hauntings have become more pronounced since the building of the water tower and the power station due to the theory that both running water and the electromagnetic fields (EMF) given off by the high-tension lines are a sort of "ghost food," giving the dead the energy to manifest into this dimension and making it easier for them to interact with the living.

Pine Hill Cemetery and "Goat Man's Grave"

St. James

Like most cemeteries, Pine Hill Cemetery is not a very scary place in the daytime, but it's a whole different story in the dark of night. Most of the graves are marked only with a single rock with nothing inscribed on them, and some aboveground graves were built by stacking sandstones around the

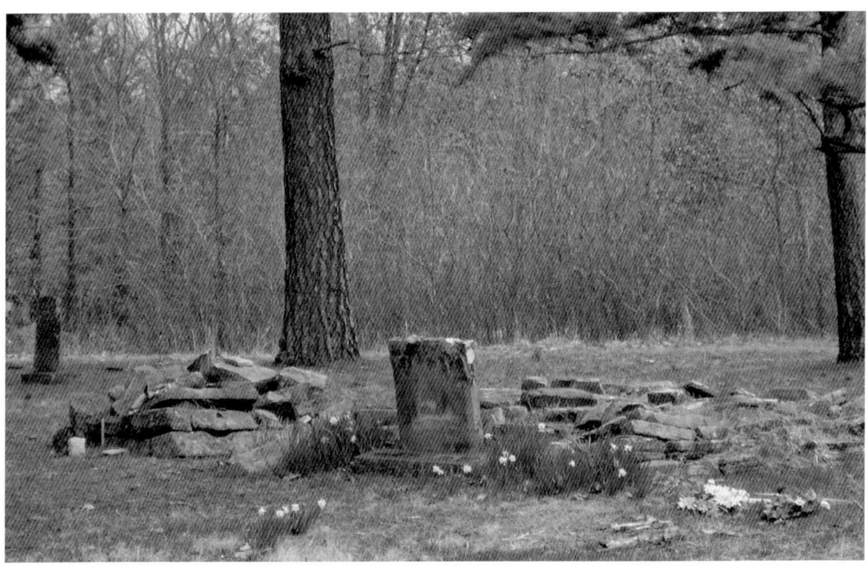

Goat Man's Grave near St. James, Missouri.

coffins. Supposedly one of the aboveground graves is what the locals believe to be that of the Goat Man. The Goat Man is said to appear out of nowhere with red glowing eyes and will chase anyone that he encounters. It is said that he can only catch you in the grass or on the gravel roads in the area but can't catch you on the pavement, as his hooves will slip. Many visitors to the cemetery report problems with electronics and camera batteries draining unusually fast, and others see shadow people darting about in the graveyard. Others experience a feeling of lightheadedness, uneasiness and a constant "swirling wind" in their ears. Many do not see the Goat Man but hear the sound of heavy hooves hitting the ground and the cry of a goat. Many have also reported the apparition of a policeman appearing out of nowhere and then disappearing, and others report a phantom car that chases them and then just disappears. Some of the paranormal activity has also been attributed to the Snelson family, who are buried in the cemetery, which is very near the site of the Snelson-Brinker Cabin.

Snelson-Brinker Cabin and Graveyard

St. James

The Snelson-Brinker log cabin was built in 1834 by Levi Snelson. Levi built, lived in and held court in the larger room of the two rooms, as he was a judge. Crawford County had no courthouses at that time. Later, Snelson sold the house and forty acres to John Brinker for $125. Adjacent to the cabin is a combination smokehouse and springhouse. The property also contains a family cemetery, known today as Brinker-Houston Cemetery, which extends some distance into the thickly wooded area beyond the graves that are visible to visitors. The cemetery is also noted by some to house the remains of buried early settlers from the Meramec Springs community, Cherokee Indians who died while passing this way on the Trail of Tears, Civil War veterans and several members of the Houston family.

Most of the Cherokees leaving Georgia followed what is today called the Northern Land Route from southeastern Tennessee across the mountains, through Nashville and Hopkinsville, Kentucky. They crossed the Ohio River near Galconda, Illinois, and continued across southern Illinois to the ice-swollen Mississippi. After crossing the Mississippi, they went northwest to Rolla before turning to the southwest to Springfield and entering northwest Arkansas. After crossing Benton and Washington Counties in Arkansas, they disbanded in northwest Indian Territory. The Northern Route continued on the road parallel to State Route 8 into Steelville. West of Steelville, the detachments followed the present-day alignment of State Route 8 to St. James. North of State Route 8, in the Woodson K. Woods State Memorial Wildlife Area, is the Snelson-Brinker Cabin, which was a stopping point for

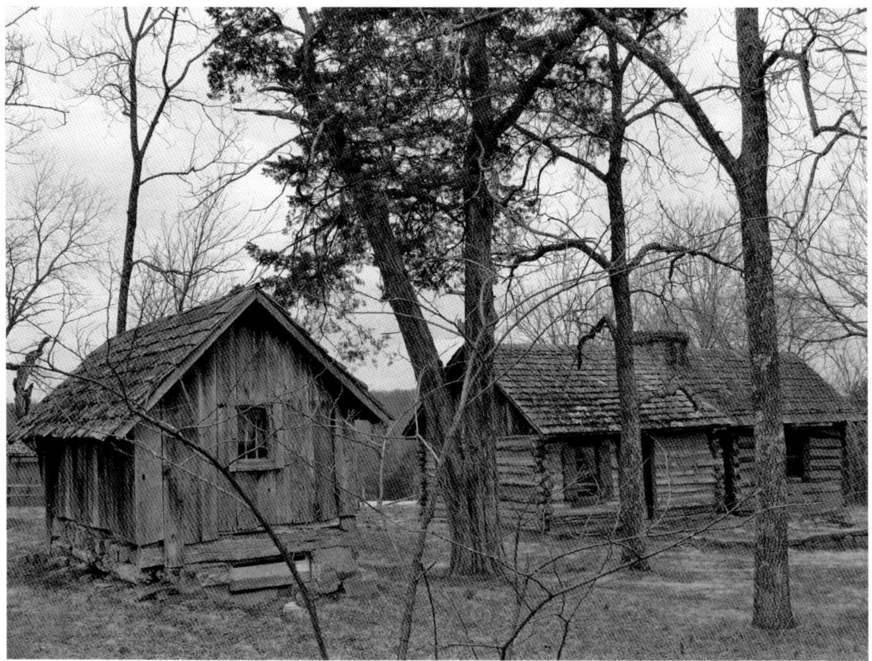

The Snelson-Brinker Cabin near St. James, Missouri.

some of the detachments. The house was owned by John Brinker in the late 1830s when the Cherokee Indians camped on the property. Four members of the Richard Taylor detachment died while at the Brinker residence and are buried in the family cemetery on the property. Although the dwelling has been altered in recent years, the site itself is significant for its associations as a known camp and burial site. Snelson-Brinker Cabin is the last Trail of Tears–certified site in Missouri, certified on October 12, 2006, and is considered by many to be a location of Indian burial grounds because of this event. It is thought that there are possibly more burials than just those known to be in the family cemetery, or perhaps these four are actually buried in a different location along the river area of the original property. More recently, the tribe council or bureau came to the property and wanted to remove its dead and return them to the burial grounds at the reservation. This request was denied, and currently the remains of any Indians buried at the cabin remain intact.

John Brinker, in the year 1837, had two daughters by the names of Vienna Jane, two years of age, and Sarah, who was just an infant at three weeks of age, as noted in some documentation. Little is known of a Mrs. Brinker; she is not mentioned in any historical documentation and no one even knows her first name or if a Mrs. actually existed at the time of the tragic event that struck the Brinker household. Brinker also had a young slave girl named Mary who cared for the children, among other duties at the cabin. She was housed in the lower portion of the spring- and smokehouse.

One day in 1837, John Brinker hitched his cart and horse and went down into the very nearby community of Meramec Springs, an ironworks town back then and historical park today, for supplies. When he returned, he found that his eldest child, Vienna Jane, was missing. Mary would give no responses or recognition that she knew anything about where the child could be. The sheriff was summoned, and a search party set out to locate the child. She was discovered in a shallow riverbed behind the cabin, deceased. Her head was bruised and battered as if she may have fallen and been knocked unconscious and possibly drowned. However, the sheriff was suspicious of how the child met her demise.

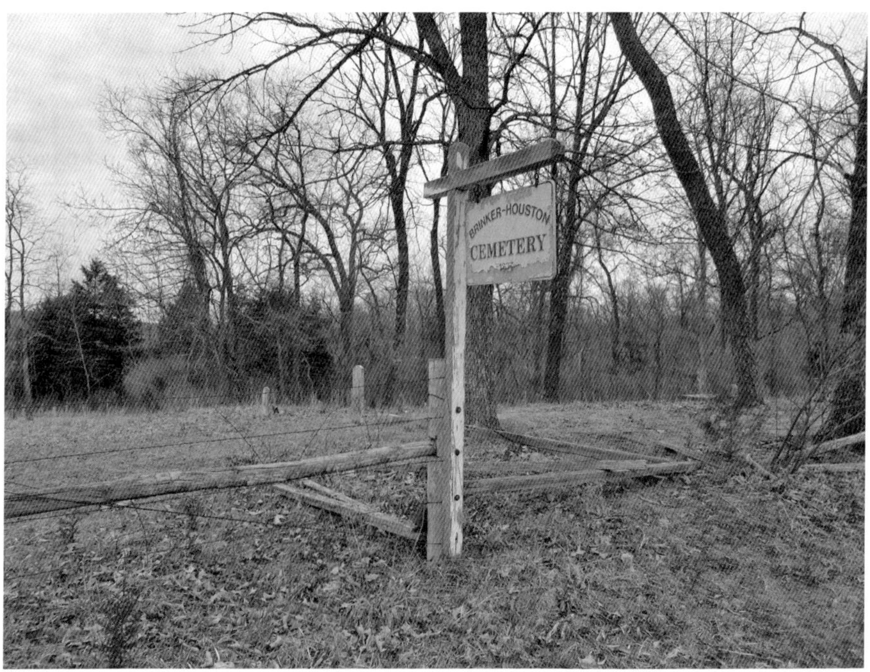

Brinker Houston Cemetery near the Snelson-Brinker Cabin.

The sheriff set up with Brinker that he would once again go into the springs for supplies, but this time they would take cover in the woods and watch the cabin. After Brinker was out of sight, they witnessed the slave girl Mary running out of the cabin with the infant, Sarah, and heading in the direction of the creek bed. They intercepted her before the infant could be harmed, and it is said that they tied her to the old tree to the right side of the cabin (if facing the cabin, the tree still remains but is dead now) and threatened to beat her if she did not talk. Mary then confessed to the killing of Vienna Jane. She stated that she tried to drown her, but the water was too shallow and she would not die, so in her words, she beat her in the head with a stick until she died. She also confessed that she was on her way to kill the remaining child, Sarah. There are different accounts as to her motive. One printed in a St. Louis newspaper stated that she did so because Brinker was going to sell her. The other version is that she had been impregnated by and given birth to Brinker's child, and the elusive Mrs. Brinker made John Brinker sell the child. Therefore, Mary committed this crime out of revenge for the loss of her own child. A news article of the time quoted Mary as being a shrewd girl who was remarkably fond of children and said that she exhibited no fear or compunction at the moment of apprehension. Mary gave her confession, signed with an x, as she was illiterate, and was taken to jail to await her indictment and trial. The news article indicates that she spent time in the Potosi Jail in Washington County. I am not sure why this would be, however, since her trial was held in Crawford County, Steelville, Missouri.

Mary was indicted on the first day. A jury of twelve white men was seated on the second day, and by the end of that day, August 18, 1837, she was convicted of first-degree murder. The very brief trial consisted of witnesses testifying against her: Thomas Shirley, William Blackwell and John B. Brinker himself. Mary's confession was deemed admissible as evidence, but caution was given to the jury by the judge that it could only be admissible as legal evidence if Mary had given the confession of her own free will without the influence of hope, fear, pain or torture. The defense offered up no evidence on behalf of Mary, according to summarizing court records, such as the sheriff's posse tying her to the tree and coercing the confession from her. I believe it is safe to say that this event most likely did take place. In that era, it was just the way things were done when it came to slaves who were owned property; essentially such actions were common. Also, to this day there have been falsehoods in the case that have stood the test of time, such as the claim that Mary was hanged from the tree in the cabin yard when found guilty

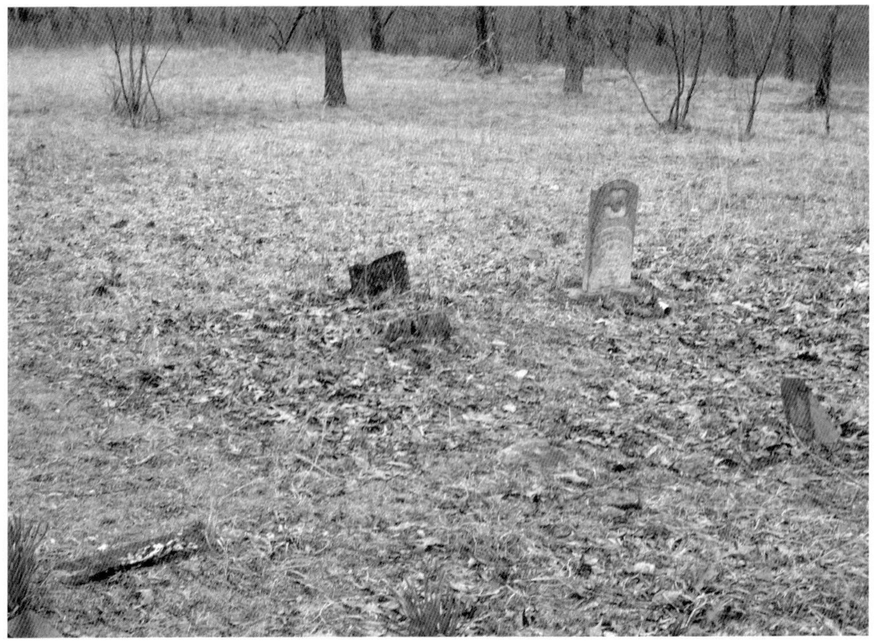

Brinker Houston Cemetery near St. James, Missouri.

of the crime. The tree has forever played an integral part in the story of Mary's case, and we know she was not hanged from this tree; therefore, the tree's stigma and true involvement in this case is very likely due to its being the location of the coerced confession of Mary. Unlike most trials of today, Mary's was pretty much one-sided. This is not to say that Mary was innocent of the crime, but it has been the basis of some speculation whether she was truly guilty.

On August 19, Judge Evans, the presiding judge on the trial, sentenced Mary to death by hanging, to be carried out on September 30, 1837. Her attorneys did make a motion for a new trial that Judge Evans denied, so they filed for appeal with the Missouri Supreme Court. The Missouri Supreme Court reversed Mary's conviction and granted her a new trial based on two grounds: inconsistent modes of death were charged in the conviction, including both beating the child to death with a stick and drowning her; and the fact that the prosecution continued to examine witnesses after agreement was made in the court that the evidence be closed, which would thereby be inflaming the jury against Mary. Her new trial was delayed over arguments of change of venue, and the trial continued into 1838. She was once again found guilty with no appeal process taken this time, and she was then hanged by the Crawford County sheriff on August 11, 1838, at the age of sixteen or seventeen. She was buried in an unmarked grave on the bluff on the north side of Steelville. Mary's execution made her the youngest known person ever put to death under Missouri authority.

As for the Brinker children, many visitors to the small cemetery have reported what feels like a small child holding their hands, and often the apparition of a small girl is seen near the cemetery and the cabin. Could these otherworldly occurrences be the result of the murdered Brinker child's ghost trying to find her loved ones?

Oak Ridge Cemetery

Doniphan

Located in Doniphan, Missouri, near the eastern edge of the Ozarks, Oak Ridge Cemetery is located on East Highway Street, just north of Fox Drive on the west side of the road. The cemetery is just northeast of downtown. Over the years, residents of Doniphan have been fascinated by the history, legends and beauty of the grave site of Belle Neal. Over her grave stands a beautifully carved statue of an angel. Legend has it that if you go to her grave at midnight on a full moon, the statue cries bloody tears and will sometimes move one of its arms. It sometimes lasts for several hours, and during this witching hour, it's said that you can walk through the graveyard and hear the faint voices of the dead.

Many people have also reported seeing the glowing white apparition of a woman in the back of the cemetery coming out of the wall of one of the old crypts and walking along a row of headstones. She carries a white cat with no head and cries mournfully. Legend says that she was a lady who lived in the area in the late 1920s. Her indoor cat ran outside, and she ran after it. When she scooped her beloved cat up in her arms in the middle of the street, they were both run over and killed by a passing beer wagon.

Old Salem Church and Cemetery

Farmington

Near the present-day city of Farmington, Missouri, the Old Salem Church and Cemetery is located ten miles north of town on Salem School Road off Highway D and HH. It is said that the original church used to have a furnace in the middle of it during the 1800s. One night, a slave boy who tended the furnace overnight fell asleep, and the entire building burned down around him. The fire was so intense that the body of the boy was never found, but being of the Christian faith, the local folks put up a tombstone for him in the cemetery just across the bridge. The church was rebuilt on the same site in the 1930s but is now condemned due to its slanting walls. The cemetery has many old gravestones, mostly of children and babies. There are also slaves buried at one end of the cemetery, but rather than being marked with tombstones, they are either unmarked or small rocks have been placed on the graves. It's believed that if you go just outside the cemetery gates at night, the sky gets strangely hazy and spirits of people can be seen walking around in the cemetery. When you turn to leave, the apparition of the young slave boy will appear at the gates just standing there staring at you. Some people have even reported that their vehicles seem to get unexplainably stuck when they try to leave this location.

Greenbrier Cemetery and the Old Spring

Marble Hill

Throughout the Civil War, both Federal and Confederate troops moved through Bollinger County, Missouri, regularly. The sentiment of much of the population of the county was with the South, making its residents particularly vulnerable to attacks by Union soldiers. Dallas (now Marble Hill), the largest town in the county and the county seat, was the frequent destination of units from both sides. Passing armies and roving guerrilla bands ravished the countryside slaughtering livestock for food, stripping fields of corn and often burning farms.

Marble Hill lies along the Old Military Road from Jackson to Greenville, a road much traveled by both Union and Confederate troops during the war. It is along the Old Military Road that visitors will find the grave of the lone Union soldier. During the war, a group of Union soldiers traveling the road stopped at a home along the way to ask for milk for a wounded soldier being carried in a wagon. The injured man died a short time later and was buried beside the road. For many years, the grave had no marker. One evening, a couple passing by the grave noticed something white. They discovered a tombstone with the inscription "W. Woods, Union Soldier. Died For His Country." No one ever learned who had placed the marker. Nearby, in Wayne County, a monument in the Cowen Cemetery marks the graves of seven Confederate soldiers, several with family ties in Bollinger County, who were shot by Union troops in Arkansas after they surrendered on May 28, 1865.

The story of the Patterson family, who lived four miles south of Marble Hill, is a vivid reminder of the savagery of the war. Here, along what was once the main trail to Zalma, William Patterson, a Confederate officer, his wife and their four young children were murdered and their bodies weighted with rocks and thrown into the deep spring on their farm. The family's house was burned, and it was several weeks before the bodies were found. They were buried on a hill near the spring. After the murders, late at night, travelers on the old trail told of seeing a blue light that seemed to float above the spring on dark stormy nights, and the spring came to be thought of as haunted. Visitors often spent the night in Marble Hill rather than traveling past the spring at night.

Greenbrier Cemetery, in southern Bollinger County, contains a mass grave discovered many years ago. An investigation of the grave determined that the plot contained the remains of Confederate soldiers. Uniforms, coats, buttons and skeletal remains were found. The remains are thought by some to be those of Confederate troops under the command of Captain Daniel McGee who were killed by Union troops in the Mingo Swamp on February 3 or 4, 1863. Although accounts vary, over twenty Confederates were killed in the encounter, while no Union soldiers were injured. Although McGee is documented in the National Archives as being a Confederate officer, Union troops at the time considered him an outlaw. Many people have reported seeing what they believe to be the apparitions of the murdered soldiers in the area.

Mayfield Cemetery and the Mystery of Eliza Jane Laycocks

Devil's Elbow

Mayfield Cemetery is located high atop a ridge near the Big Piney River in Pulaski County, Missouri, five miles off J Highway in the Mark Twain National Forest. It also leads to the spot of an interesting mystery known to many in the area. On this road in the Ozark hills just up from Mayfield Cemetery is a roadside grave belonging to Eliza Jane Laycocks Thomas. I first heard about this location referred to as the "Witch's Grave" by locals while researching for this book. Locals share many theories as to why she is buried outside the cemetery, with the most prevalent being that she was a witch due to the amount of paranormal occurrences that have been reported near her grave over the years. Not much is known about Eliza Jane, but speculation would make one think that she was probably never referred to as a witch in her time but her lonely grave has made her the subject of a rural myth in the Pulaski County area. I am sure that the road may have changed over the past century, but being on top of an Ozarks Mountain ridge, I doubt that it has changed drastically. Most of the gravestones in the Mayfield Cemetery not far from Eliza's final resting place are from the same era.

Few facts are known about Eliza Jane Laycocks. However, she does show up in the 1880 United States Federal Census. According to this document, her home was the counties of Miller and Phelps, Missouri. During the time of the census, she was fifteen, which would have made her birth year 1865. She was born in Missouri, the daughter of William A. and Susan A. Laycocks. Her father was from Tennessee and her mother was from Missouri. Using the 1880 census as a reference, one would think that she was the oldest of at least four children. Also living in the household were Willey Laycocks, age twelve; William Laycocks, age ten; and George Laycocks, age eight.

According to a handmade marker nailed to a tree above her grave site, she was the wife of Henry and died circa 1897 at the age of thirty-two. Some questions remain unanswered: why was Eliza Jane Laycocks Thomas buried alone alongside a roadway? And why does she seemingly haunt this area to this day?

One of the more popular stories states that Eliza and her husband, Henry, lived in a cabin in the woods only a couple hundred yards back from where Eliza's grave is located. Her husband died of unknown causes and friends tried to get Eliza to move away, but she refused, as that area was her home. Apparently an undetermined time later, she became sick and died. She was found by friends who lived nearby and was buried on the land that she so loved during her lifetime.

We may never know the secrets that her grave holds, but for many who visit her final resting place there is often a feeling of overwhelming sadness and loneliness that seems to follow even after they have left the vicinity.

Just up the road from Eliza's grave in Mayfield Cemetery, the oldest legible dated stone is that of Joshua Davis, who died on August 30, 1879, at approximately seventy-four years old. The most recent legible stone belongs to Louisa Virginia Deer, wife of John W. Deer, who passed away in 1913. At one time, Mayfield Cemetery was well kept, and pictures survive of a Decoration Day there. Over time, most of the relatives of those buried here have either passed away themselves or moved away, and it is no longer a gathering place on Decoration Day. Today, Mayfield Cemetery seems very desolate and abandoned with the exception of a few lost souls who still reside there in spirit. Many who visit Mayfield Cemetery have witnessed strange lights in the cemetery and in the nearby woods. Mists and obscure shadows have also been reported in and around the cemetery. This area is also used as a campground, so don't be surprised if you see someone camping out there. This is definitely an active site. While you're there, don't forget to stop off and pay your respects to Eliza Jane Laycocks Thomas.

Hrbitov Sv Vaclava Catholic Cemetery

Karlin

Hrbitov Sv Vaclava Catholic Cemetery, which translates from Czech as St. Wenceslaus Cemetery, is located in what once was Karlin, Missouri. Today, Karlin is virtually a ghost town, as there is about one family left near where the town once stood. Karlin was a small railroad town in a Bohemian settlement about four miles south of Bolivar. Originally it was called Tremont, but when the seven sons of Francka arrived in 1890, they changed the name to Karlin in honor of a city in the extreme northern part of Bohemia. The post office was changed from Tremont to Karlin in 1903. St. Wenceslaus Church in Karlin was established in 1904 and was placed on the inactive list in May 1965 because of a shortage of priests to staff all the churches and missions in the diocese. Most of the town and its history are now lost with time—with the exception of the old cemetery that still remains.

Many in the area of the old cemetery claim to see dark shadowy figures inside and around the cemetery. Reports have also stated that crying, laughter and eerie sounds can be heard throughout the cemetery and the surrounding forests. One local resident who lives near the old cemetery claimed that a dark figure would appear in her yard at around 2:00 a.m. knocking things over and going through her trash. Her dogs would usually get riled up and bark at it for about an hour every night. One dog was apparently kicked or attacked by the shadowy figure. One night the dog's owner heard it being struck, followed by a sharp yelp. After the incident, the dog seemed to limp a bit and cowered in fear for days.

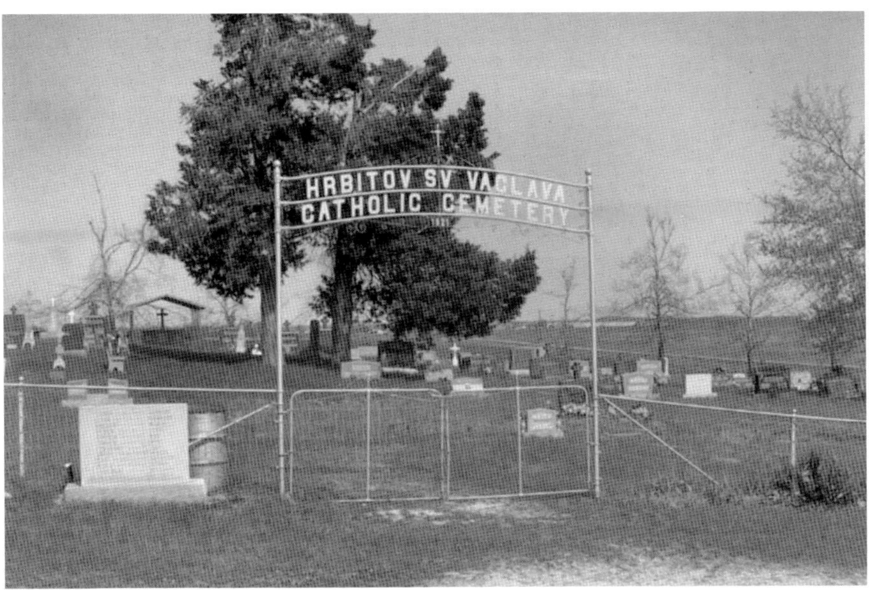

St. Wenceslaus Cemetery, Karlin, Missouri.

Many in the area believe that the shadowy figure could be the spirit of Karlin's most renowned resident, Charles Andera. When Charles Andera died in 1929, he left behind a unique legacy: hundreds of ornate, distinctive cast metal crosses that mark the final resting places of Roman Catholic Czech Americans in no fewer than twelve states across the country. His beautiful grave markers have been found in cemeteries from Prague, Oklahoma, to Bohemia, New York, from Pisek, North Dakota, to Hallettsville, Texas. Almost exclusively, these monuments are in Czech Catholic graveyards.

In addition to his wonderful work, Andera left us with a number of questions. Where did he learn his many skills, where did he have his intricate crosses cast, how did he market them and how many more are there that we don't know about? Those questions are all begging answers. An effort is now underway to resolve them and to locate and catalogue all of his wonderful grave marker crosses.

Andera came to this country with his parents and several siblings in the early 1860s from Hrobska Zahradka (Garden of the Graves), a small village near Tabor, Bohemia. Its name derived from the ancient burial mounds near which it was located. After a short stay in Toronto, Canada, the family settled on a farm near Spillville, in Winneshiek County, Iowa. There, in

1875, Charles married Barbara Dostal, the daughter of a wagon maker. Where he lived in the interim is unknown. Was it perhaps with an older half brother near Charles City, Iowa, who had trained in Vienna, Austria, as a furniture maker? When the question came up long after his death, no one had the answer.

Now a skilled carpenter and cabinetmaker, Charles Andera opened a furniture store next to his small house in Spillville. His work included the construction of the communion rail and other wooden appointments in Spillville's St. Wenceslaus Church. Bells of the clock he installed in its steeple sounded on the quarter hour and could be heard for miles. Commuting by bicycle, he crafted alters in the Catholic churches in nearby Fort Atkinson and Protivin. He also made burial caskets.

The earliest crosses in existence in the Spillville cemetery were made from wagon makers' strap iron and may have been the product of Jan Dostal, Andera's father-in-law. Was this connection perhaps what gave Charles Andera his cross-making start? There would have also been wooden crosses of oak, a common practice that, in his native land, went back several centuries. An early photo (another of his skills) by Andera shows one wooden cross and two of cast metal. Of the latter, one is relatively plain and may have been his first design in cast metal. The other, which in later photos he identified as #1, is the first model he decorated with a religious symbol. Although none of his wooden crosses is known to exist today, they are mentioned in a history of Karlin, where he lived after the turn of the century until his death.

Strangely, there appears to be no pattern in the manner in which Andera marked his crosses. Some simply have his initials, "C.A."; others include his initials or name, the words "Spillville, IA" or "Tremont, Mo." and may include the date of manufacture. Some, on the back of the heart-shaped inscription plate, are marked "No. 5" or carry the outline of a cross. Many monuments otherwise identical to the marked crosses are unmarked.

Charles Andera sculpted his crosses from wood and plaster of Paris and then sent this pattern to a foundry to have it cast. The crosses, of which there were several sizes, as well as the small statues that adorn two of his designs, he carved from wood. The inscription plates he may have cast himself.

The Andera grave marker crosses are rich in symbolism. His #1 was adorned with skull and crossbones. (This did not indicate that the deceased had died from poison, as one schoolchild surmised, but was an image commonly displayed by Czech Catholics in centuries past as a reminder of man's mortality.) This style was also available with an abstract design. Other symbols and decorations the cross maker utilized include angels, cherubs, crucifixes, the Lamb of God, statues of Jesus and the Virgin Mother, the crown of thorns, quatrefoils and trefoils. Andera crosses have been found throughout the United States in Iowa, Minnesota, Wisconsin, Michigan, New York, North Dakota, South Dakota, Nebraska, Oklahoma, Kansas, Missouri and Texas.

We will most likely never know if it's Andera's spirit that haunts the old cemetery and nearby woods, but for many souls living near the old cemetery, the spirit of Charles Andera still lives on.

Old Carney Cemetery

Jenkins

Situated near Jenkins, Missouri, is the Old Carney Cemetery, where many folks have reported seeing and experiencing strange things for many years. Most notably, folks have reported seeing what appear to be the apparitions of a male and a female wandering about the cemetery grounds. Others have reported seeing strange lights that swirl through the air just to disappear into the night, and some have reported seeing a strange misty fog that moves throughout the area. Could these otherworldly occurrences be partially attributed to a double murder that occurred near the cemetery well over a century ago? This horrific series of events resulted in the only reported lynching Barry County, Missouri, has ever experienced.

The site of the brutal murders, which took place early on a Saturday evening, December 4, 1869, was a small country store operated by Jack Carney and his bride of ten months, Mary Cordelia, in the village of Schell Knob just west of the Stone-Barry County line. When a post office was established at this location on July 12, 1872, the postal department dropped—whether by accident or design it is not known—the "c" from Schell, and since then the town has been known as "Shell Knob."

The slaying took place in a double log building located about four hundred feet west and slightly south of the present schoolhouse site at Shell Knob. Shortly after the marriage of the young couple, the Carneys had obtained the double log structure, one end of which was used as a residence and the other end of which was used as a store building. It stood just south of the present roadbed of Highway 39 in what is now the eastern edge of Shell

Knob. Carney was twenty years of age and Mary Cordelia was twenty-one when they were both viciously murdered.

The murder took place about dark on Saturday evening but was not discovered until Sunday afternoon, when a resident of the community went to the store to pick up a package of goods he had purchased the day before. The door was not fastened, and on entering, the visitor found Carney lying dead on the floor. He had been shot twice, both bullets having entered his head near his mouth, and apparently had died immediately. Mary Cordelia had been shot in the upper chest, and when the shot was fired, her clothing took fire and was entirely consumed down to her waist in flames.

An inquest was held on the afternoon of December 8 and a verdict given that Jackson Carney and wife came to their death from pistol fire. On Tuesday afternoon, the husband and wife were buried side by side in the same grave and the same coffin. There were more persons present at this funeral than ever assembled at any funeral in this county. The murdered husband was well respected by all who knew him. He was known all through this section of country to be a good citizen and a kind husband; no man ever lived a more honorable or peaceful life. Those who knew him loved and respected him. His wife was one of the best women, kind, dutiful and affectionate. It is thought that neither husband nor wife had an enemy in the world. The neighbors and acquaintances were excited to the very highest extent by this sad occurrence. Nothing but seeing the murderer punished could satisfy them.

Patrons who had visited the store on Saturday immediately voiced their suspicions of a young man named George Moore, a twenty-eight-year-old ne'er-do-well who had been reared in large part by the Carney family. Word was immediately sent to Sheriff John H. Moore (no relation) in Cassville to arrest young Moore if he should be found in that area.

George Moore had spent a large portion of the day Saturday lounging about Carney's store and had been seen there about sundown that evening. Moore and Carney had been acquainted from childhood. About a year prior to the slaying, George Moore had robbed an elderly man in the neighborhood and immediately fled to Arkansas, where his mother resided. At the time of the robbery, he was working for John Carney, the father of Jack Carney, and while there was sent by John Carney to take the elderly man, who had gotten drunk and was not in a condition to be trusted alone with his team of horses, home. While going home with the old man, Moore robbed him and then fled. Nothing was heard from Moore until a few days before the double slaying, when he made his appearance at Gadfly (a now extinct town located just west of Purdy), in Barry County. He remained there two or three days and then left, going directly to Carney's store, where he arrived on Saturday about 11:00 a.m. Moore spent the entire afternoon at Carney's store, and apparently the two enjoyed the afternoon visit, even indulging in a friendly scuffle. The patrons of the store that afternoon later noted that there was every appearance of friendship between the two young men, but as soon as the last visitor had left the store, Moore got down to the business for which he had apparently made the visit.

A few minutes after he was last seen at Carney's, between sundown and dark, three pistol shots were heard in the direction of the store by a neighbor who resided about a quarter of a mile away.

About two hours later, Moore sought lodging for the night at a house about nine miles from the store in the direction of Cassville and remained there overnight. He was traveling by horseback. On Sunday, he attended church at the Homer schoolhouse near Cassville, and on Monday, the sheriff arrested Moore about a mile and a half south of Cassville and lodged him in the county jail.

At the time of the arrest, Moore was wearing the hat of the murdered victim and had Carney's revolver strapped around him, while Moore's hat and a pistol were found in the store where the slayings occurred. On his person was found $201, which had been taken from the store. The money was found a little of it in each of his pockets, with some in the lining of his pants, his coat and his vest and here and there a bill pinned to the inside of his clothing. Shortly before the slayings occurred, Mary Cordelia Carney had dyed some woolen material with a yellow dye. In making change at the store, she had handled some of the bills while her hands were wet with the dye, and the dye had gotten on some of the paper money. After his capture, some of the money that Moore was found to be carrying had traces of the yellow dye on it.

Sheriff Moore transported young Moore to the county jail, which was a new jail and had been built and accepted by the county on October 10, 1867, some two years earlier. It was built of log construction and was a rather formidable structure. It had been built, as per the order of the county court, "six feet from the county courthouse." The Barry County Courthouse, a two-story brick structure constructed in 1856, was located in the center of the public square in Cassville on the site of the present Barry County Courthouse.

Carney was a member of one of the early pioneer families of Barry County. Thomas G. Carney and his family settled in extreme east central

Barry County in the 1830s. He was the father of John Carney and the grandfather of Jackson Carney. John Carney, father of the slain storekeeper, had attained a considerable degree of prominence, having served as county judge from 1863 to 1868. As a result of the prominence of the family and the ruthless nature of the murders, indignation was at a high point in the eastern part of the county.

On Monday evening, a large company of friends and relatives of the victims converged on the county seat with the announced purpose of taking the prisoner out of jail and executing him. The sheriff only managed to save him by secretly taking the prisoner out of jail and running him to the country.

The deceased victims were buried on Tuesday. On Wednesday, it is estimated that some two hundred men, virtually all of whom were residents of the vicinity of the crime, gathered for what was understood by the sheriff to be the purpose of hearing the trial. Having been assured that the prisoner was to have a trial, the sheriff was shocked when he was surrounded by several men demanding the keys to the jail.

The sheriff, fearing for his own life, finally succumbed to their demands and gave them the keys. Several wooden goods boxes were procured from nearby stores and placed under an extending arm from the bell post, which stood at the southeast corner of the square. Suspended from the bell post was a bell that had been purchased by the public-spirited citizens of Cassville in 1868 and was used chiefly for the purpose of calling the students to school and the worshipers to church. It was from this post that young Moore met his doom.

The lynching occurred shortly before the noon hour on Wednesday, when Moore was placed atop the boxes with a rope around his neck, the other end of which was fastened on the end of the extension to the bell post. Before he was hanged, Moore was requested and given time to confess but refused; he did not appear to be frightened in the least. It is very probable that he was so hardened to crime that death caused no fear in him. He refused to say anything, and as legend has it, the boxes were suddenly jerked from beneath the prisoner by Watt Carney, who was a brother of the slain merchant. The body was left hanging throughout the afternoon and at dark was taken down and transported to Oak Hill Cemetery, at the east edge of the Cassville city limits, and there buried in an unmarked grave.

It is interesting to note that on February 20, 1877, the bell was donated to the Cassville School District and was removed from its post on the public square to a school building that had just been constructed. It continued to

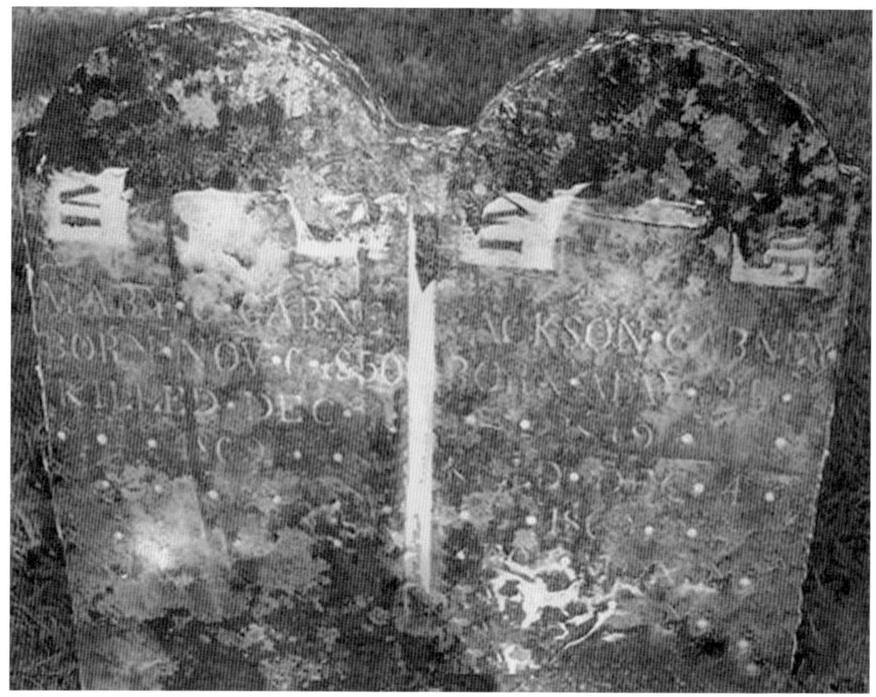

The double grave of murder victims Jackson and Mary Cordelia Carney in the Old Carney Cemetery in Jenkins, Missouri.

do service for the school district until 1939, but after twenty-seven years of retirement, the bell was enshrined in 1966 on the school grounds in Cassville. This was not done for any significance as to the lynching but simply because it was the first and only bell ever used by the Cassville schools.

Jackson and Cordelia Carney are buried in a double grave in the Old Carney Cemetery near the Stone-Barry County line in eastern Barry County south of Wheelerville. Could the wandering apparitions reported to be seen at the Old Carney Cemetery be those of Jackson and Mary Cordelia seeking out each other or possibly seeking out some sort of justice for their short lives coming to such an abrupt and tragic ending? I suppose we'll never really know for sure.

Slagle Cemetery

Chillicothe

The legend of Slagle's Mill and the nearby cemetery has been part of Livingston County folklore for more than one hundred years. Joseph Slagle was born in Augusta County, Virginia, on September 26, 1810. He was the youngest of twelve children of George Slagle, who owned considerable property, operated a mill and ran a distillery.

Joseph Slagle came to Missouri in 1830 and sold goods at Cox's Mill, which he bought soon afterward. The mill was on Medicine Creek, then the only water mill in northwest Missouri. In 1846, he was elected to the official bench of the county and was also justice of the peace for many years. He was one of the largest property holders in the county, having in his possession some 1,400 acres of land. A county history states that Joseph Slagle was married five times, first on January 27, 1832, to Catherine Long of Ohio, who died on July 6, 1841, leaving a son, Columbus Genoa. Slagle married Miss Catherine Stone of West Virginia on November 22, 1843, but she died on August 24, 1844. His third marriage took place on May 5, 1845, to Miss Sarah Littlepage, who died in September 1846, leaving a daughter, Susan Catherine. He married his fourth wife, Miss Crawford of Illinois, in 1848. She died in 1849. He was married a fifth time to Mrs. Lottie P. Ellis of Indiana in 1869. One son resulted from that marriage, Joseph Lee Slagle.

A history of Caldwell and Livingston County was published in 1886 by the St. Louis National Historical Company from "the most authentic official and private sources." It contains an account of the first homicide

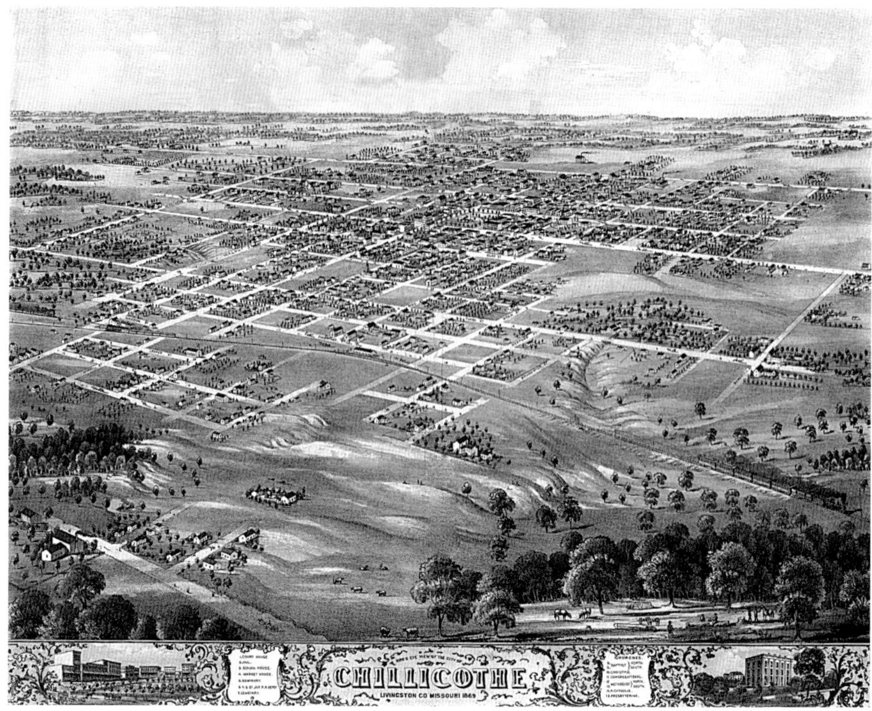

An old map of Chillicothe, Missouri. *Courtesy of the Library of Congress.*

in Livingston County—the killing of Benjamin Collins by Joseph Slagle. This occurred on April 19, 1853, when Slagle was married to Elizabeth Crawford, who was a half sister of Benjamin Collins. Collins at this time lived in Quincy, Illinois, where "he was connected with a 'negro show,' and led a low disreputable life generally…he was regarded as a malicious, evil-disposed person, of a quarrelsome nature, especially when intoxicated, as was frequently the case."

When Collins heard that his half sister had married Slagle, he "flew into a great passion, and swore that he was coming 'right over to Missouri and kill Slagle.'" Collins seemed incensed against Slagle because the latter had been married twice before marrying his sister and because he was somewhat older than she was. Collins uttered threats against Slagle, "declaring he had killed his first two wives, and 'he shan't live to kill my sister.'"

On the morning of April 19, Collins left a boardinghouse near Chillicothe and started into town with Thomas Gilkison. Collins was unarmed. That same morning, Slagle started from home to hunt for one of his cattle that had strayed. He was on horseback and carried a double-barreled gun. He soon overtook Collins and Gilkison. Mr. Gilkison testified to the following:

> *We had got but a short distance from Mrs. Sapp's house till we seen Mr. Slagle. This man that got killed remarked to me, "Will he shoot?" I told the man that I did not think he would shoot if he met him friendly. When he met Mr. Slagle he spoke and bid him "good morning," Mr. Slagle bid him "good morning." Collins asked Mr. Slagle: "How do you come on." Mr. Slagle's reply was: "Ben, my life has been at stake long enough." As he spoke these two words he cocked his gun and shot. As he did not kill him the first shot, he shot again; the last shot killed him dead on the ground.*

Gilkison also said that after Slagle had killed Collins, " He seemed greatly affected, 'shedding tears' and declaring 'I would not have done it, but I had to. I would as soon have shot my own brother.'"

Slagle surrendered himself and was indicted by the grand jury. He was acquitted, "the jury believing from the evidence, as did a majority of the community, that he had killed Collins from motives altogether proper and justifiable."

There is a major discrepancy in some of this information. The "Miss Crawford" whom Slagle married in 1848 died in 1849, so she could not have been around in 1853 when Joseph Slagle killed Benjamin Collins. Some people believe that Collins came to Missouri to take revenge on Slagle because Slagle had married the sister (Elizabeth Crawford) of his dead wife. Collins was afraid that this other half sister, Elizabeth, would be killed by Joseph Slagle as her sister supposedly had been. If this is indeed true, Joseph Slagle would have had six wives.

It is believed by many locals that the body of the murdered Collins is buried beneath the road that runs past the Slagle Cemetery, but there is no valid evidence that this is where Collins's body is actually interred. The graves of Joseph Slagle's wives and children are still there, along with his own, and the Slagle Cemetery is said to be very haunted, according to locals as well as several paranormal researchers. There was also a very old bridge on the property that was said to be haunted. The current owners of the property have reported hearing mysterious whispers on the bridge, and sightings of Slagle are very common around the cemetery and where the mill stood. One of Slagle's wives supposedly hanged herself from the old bridge after the mysterious death of one of her children, and the transparent figure of a

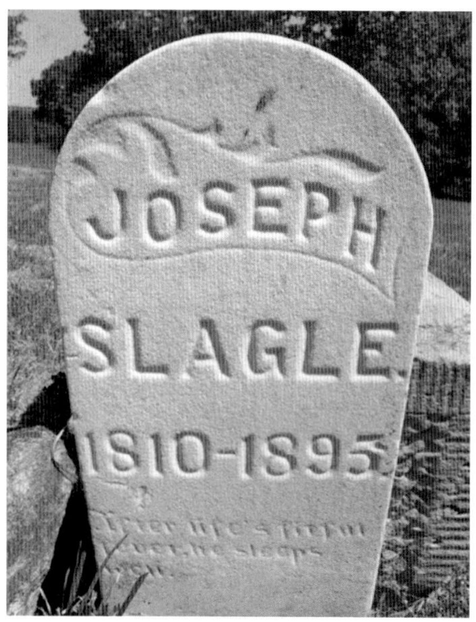

The grave of Joseph Slagle in the Slagle Cemetery, Chillicothe, Missouri.

young woman in an old-fashioned dress is still reported to this day wandering about the cemetery and near where the bridge once stood. There were satanic symbols painted on the bridge and lots of evidence of vandalism, as it was a popular place for teenagers to hang out at night and party. There are many stories of several people who were mysteriously pushed off the bridge and injured when no one was standing around or near them. But too many people were injured, and the bridge was made off limits and has since been torn down by the property owners.

Another tale of Slagle Cemetery that has been circulated in the Ozarks involves two men who went quail hunting one day and two youths who, by unfortunate chance, unknowingly came across them. On their way back home after a bountiful day of hunting, the two hunters came across the Old Slagle Cemetery and thought it the perfect place to stop and drop off their heavy load of kill for the day, as they still needed to go check on a deer-lick that they had placed nearby. They figured that the old cemetery would be a safe place to leave their claim, as nobody in the area would ever venture near the old burying place due to all the tales of ghosts and such that surrounded it. Just after dusk, on their way back to the cemetery, they shot two more quail and thought that most fortunate.

Upon arriving back at the old graveyard, they dropped off the quail that they had just shot outside the cemetery gate and decided they would go inside to divide up the day's bounty and part ways back home. Unknown to the hunters, two local boys had just arrived at the cemetery to try to see any of the ghosts that they had heard tales of all their short lives. Upon arriving just outside the cemetery walls, the two boys, not aware of the two hunters, quickly crouched down when they heard voices saying, "Let's just divide them up. You take one and I'll take one and you take one and I'll take one." Quite frightened, the boys then heard a voice saying, "We'll go outside the gate and get the other two." Well, the boys thought it meant them, so one boy shouted to the other, "Run! Run! They're coming to get us!" Frantically running through the woods, the boys made it back home and told their folks what they had experienced down at the old cemetery. Their parents told them that what they had experienced was the devil and the good lord dividing up souls in the cemetery and they were ready to come out and get them and they should never go there again!

So, if you're ever in the vicinity of Slagle Cemetery, stop in and say hello to Mr. Slagle and his family…if you're brave enough.

Springfield National Cemetery

Springfield

Springfield National Cemetery was established in 1867 on prairie land south of Springfield, Missouri. Today, the cemetery's eighteen acres are bounded by residential neighborhoods and commercial areas. Initially created as a final resting place for Union soldiers who died at the Battle of Wilson's Creek near Springfield, the cemetery now contains the remains of veterans from other wars, including the Revolutionary War, Spanish-American War and World War II. The Springfield National Cemetery also includes a six-acre portion established by the Confederate Cemetery Association in 1871. An act of Congress in 1911 authorized the secretary of war to accept the Confederate cemetery as part of the Springfield National Cemetery.

Springfield lies on the Springfield Plateau of the Ozark Mountains, which gives the city its nickname, "Gateway of the Ozarks." First settled in 1829 by John Polk Campbell, the area quickly became an established settlement with stores, mills and a post office and was incorporated as a town in 1838.

Although Missouri voted to stay in the Union, Confederate sympathies ran strong throughout the state. On August 10, 1861, the first major Civil War engagement west of the Mississippi River occurred ten miles south of Springfield. More than five thousand Union troops and twelve thousand Confederate forces clashed at Wilson's Creek. The battle ended in a Confederate victory, but disorganization and bad planning prevented Southern forces from capitalizing on their success. The battle is significant, marking the first death of a Union general in combat;

Brigadier General Nathaniel Lyon died during a Union charge, felled by a Confederate bullet.

After the Civil War, the City of Springfield purchased eighty acres of prairie for a cemetery and granted the U.S. government the privilege of selecting a plot for a national cemetery. Five acres were selected on the highest ground and purchased for $37.50 an acre. The Springfield National Cemetery was officially established in 1867, and many of the men who died in the Battle of Wilson's Creek were buried there. Additionally, the remains of Union troops buried in several Missouri counties were removed and reinterred in the new cemetery.

In 1871, a Confederate cemetery was established adjacent to the national cemetery, containing roughly 6.0 acres total with an area of 2.7 acres enclosed by a wall. In March 1911, Congress authorized the secretary of war to accept the Confederate cemetery as part of the Springfield National Cemetery. A deed restriction prevented the burial of anyone other than Confederate military veterans within the boundaries of the old Confederate cemetery.

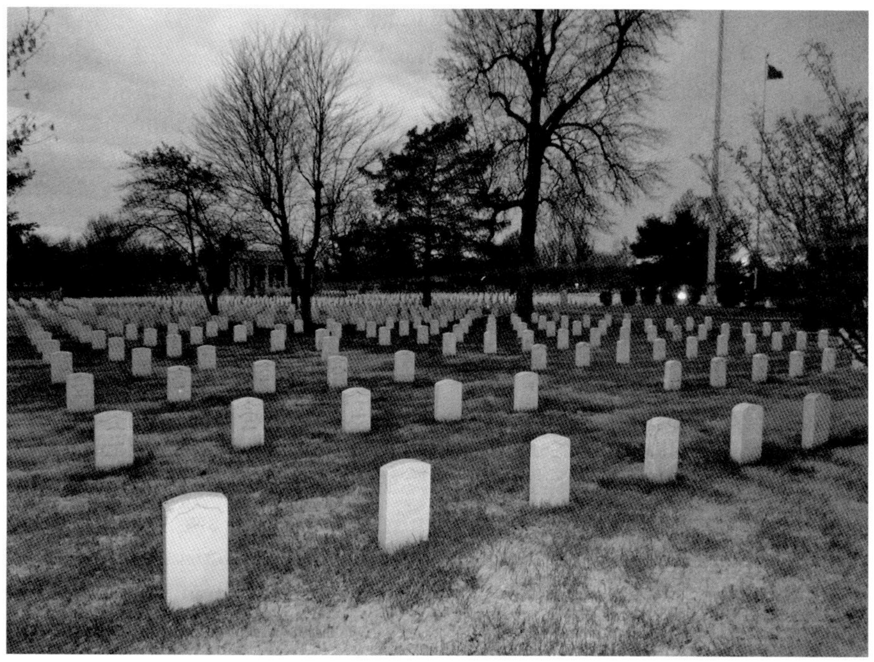

Springfield National Cemetery, Springfield, Missouri.

After World War II, the Department of the Army expanded the national cemetery, receiving approval from the Confederate Cemetery Association to use areas within the boundaries of the old Confederate cemetery but outside the enclosed area. In the 1980s, given the many unoccupied graves within the area restricted for Confederate burials, the Department of Veterans Affairs and the Confederate Cemetery Association of Missouri agreed to allow burials of all veterans in the area within the enclosure wall. In 1984, the Daughters of the Confederacy dedicated a plaque on a monument in the old Confederate section, stating that the area's "use by all veterans and their dependents serves as a symbol of unification of purpose for memorializing those who have honorably served this great nation."

Also located on the grounds of the cemetery is a rectangular stone-block rostrum. Built between the Confederate and Union portions of the cemetery, the rostrum resembles a miniature Greek temple and features speakers' lecterns on both sides for patriotic and memorial observances. Bronze plaques on the rostrum's south side face toward the Confederate graves. One plaque references the Confederate soldiers buried there and the battles in which they died, notably the Battle of Wilson's Creek. The other plaques state the establishment dates of the Confederate cemetery and the installation of the cemetery's carillon in 1979. On the rostrum's north side, facing Union graves, a single plaque is inscribed with a memorial to the veterans of the Vietnam War.

Several large commemorative monuments stand on the cemetery's grounds. Two are located just east of the administration building. The oldest is a memorial honoring Brigadier General Nathaniel Lyon, the commanding officer at the Battle of Wilson's Creek and the first Union general to die in the Civil War. The twelve-foot-tall monument, erected in 1888 by the citizens of Springfield, is a marble pillar topped with a knight's helmet, battle-axe and wreath. Near the Lyon monument, a Union memorial stands twenty-five feet tall. Erected in 1907 in accordance with the bequest of local doctor T.J. Bailey, it features a life-sized statue of an infantry soldier and is inscribed with a commemoration honoring the Union dead. The other side of the monument has an inscription stating that the monument was "erected under the provisions of the last will of Dr. Thomas Bailey to show his love for the Union and its gallant defenders."

Commissioned by the United Confederate Veterans of Missouri in 1901, Italian sculptor Chevalier Trentanove created a bronze figure of a Confederate soldier to honor the Confederate soldiers of Missouri and General Sterling Price, a former governor of Missouri and the Confederate

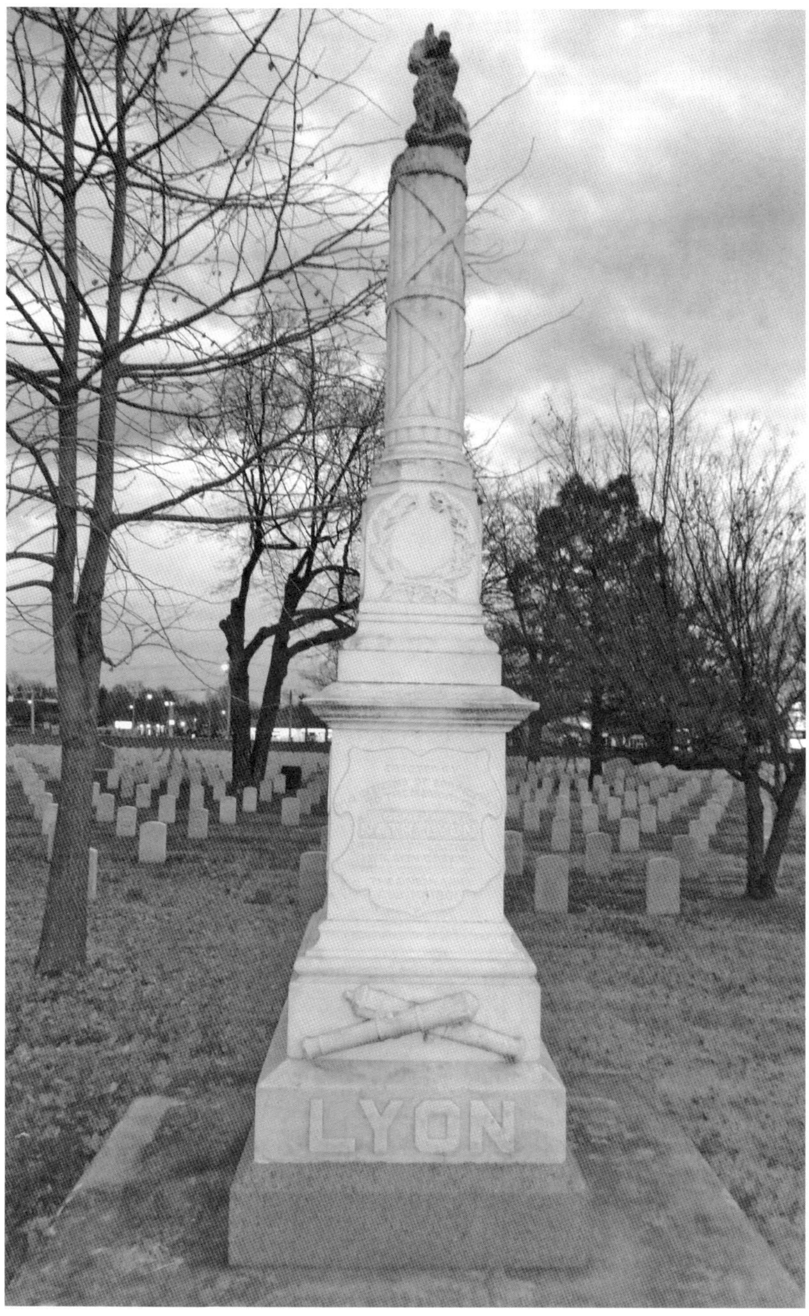

General Lyon's marker in Springfield National Cemetery.

commander at the Battle of Wilson's Creek. The front of the monument features a bronze bas-relief portrait of Price. Also located within the old Confederate cemetery grounds is a granite marker, placed in 1958 by the Daughters of the Confederacy, honoring the unknown Confederate dead at the Battle of Wilson's Creek.

Erected in recent years, other monuments at the Springfield National Cemetery include a granite and bronze memorial to those who died in the attack on Pearl Harbor in 1941. The Pearl Harbor Survivors Association dedicated the memorial in 1992. In 1999, the Sons and Daughters of the American Revolution installed a granite monument in honor of those who died in the Revolutionary War. A Revolutionary War veteran, Private William Freeman, is buried at Springfield National Cemetery. Freeman was a North Carolina militia member who served as a scout for General George Washington. Freeman's grave is located near the General Lyon Memorial.

Other notable burials in Springfield National Cemetery include five Buffalo Soldiers. Members of African American army regiments created after the Civil War, the Buffalo Soldiers protected settlers moving west, built and renovated army posts and camps and maintained law and order in the western expanses of the country.

Springfield National Cemetery is the final resting place of five recipients of the Medal of Honor, the nation's highest military decoration, given for "conspicuous gallantry and intrepidity at the risk of his life above and beyond the call of duty."

The Springfield National Cemetery is host to more than a few lingering spirits as well, according to some people. Late-night visitors to the cemetery have reported seeing gravestones that appeared to glow in the dark. Yet others have reported finding strange anomalies in photographs they took while inside the cemetery grounds. On occasion, some photographs even show what appears to be an apparition or form of some long-dead solider standing among the tombstones. Others have even reported having interactions with what they describe as a Civil War soldier who seems on the surface to be a real person but then just vanishes into thin air.

Spanish Fort Cemetery

Mount Vernon

A small, secluded cemetery, Spanish Fort Cemetery is a lovely old place out in the country near Mount Vernon dating back to 1880. Located along the Spring Creek at an old confluence or split on the creek up on a ridge in Lawrence County, it is the first evidence of ancient mound builders in the Ozarks. Lawrence County was organized in 1845 and named for James Lawrence, a naval officer from the War of 1812 known for his statement, "Don't give up the ship." As the name implies, the area was thought by many locals to contain the remnants of a fort established by Spanish explorers, but the general consensus today is that it's actually an ancient Indian mound. If you visit Spanish Fort Cemetery, you'll find that it is overgrown with grass and weeds most of the year, as it is no longer maintained. Evidence of the mound is still visible to this day and can be located by the stone marker erected atop it.

On Sunday, October 12, 1930, an appropriate marker provided by the University Club of Springfield, Missouri, was dedicated. Dr. F.T. H'Doubler delivered the dedicatory address, and the marker was unveiled by Dr. E.M. Shepard. Made of granite, the stone marker is six feet high, two feet wide and eight inches thick. Little, if any, vandalism is evident after nearly a century, probably due to the isolated location. The text on the marker reads as follows:

> *Fort Ancient, believed to have been constructed by a group of eastward migrating Mound Builders, a band of Indians probably long antedating*

the Osages, on their way to what is now Ohio. These earthworks are a small replica of the great Fort Ancient in Ohio, where this prehistoric group reached its greatest culmination. This tribe probably had its village in the valley and used these fortifications for defence. First pioneers describe the walls as originally about 5 ft high and the moat 2 ft deep. Springfield University Club Historical Marker No. 16. Erected Oct. 1930.

On the reverse side of the marker, possibly to placate the local folk, is inscribed: "Locally known as the Old Spanish Fort." This refers to the fact that the site was formerly known as Spanish Fort, particularly by the local residents of the region. It was designated Fort Ancient in 1930 after a study of more than forty years by Dr. E.M. Shepard, an archaeologist and geologist.

Dr. Shepard had been employed by the State of Missouri to write about the geology of the district. From his prolonged study, it seems probable that the Mound Builder Indians were the creators of Fort Ancient and that the Spanish only occupied it for a short period during the 1500s. The Mound

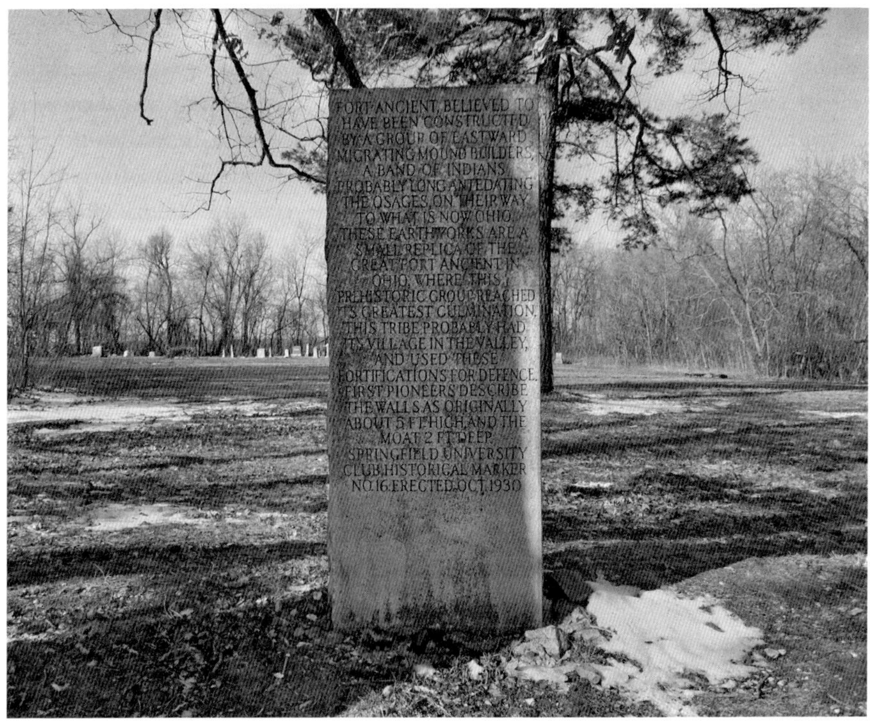

A marker at Spanish Fort Cemetery, Mount Vernon, Missouri. *Courtesy of Shane Wade Corkren.*

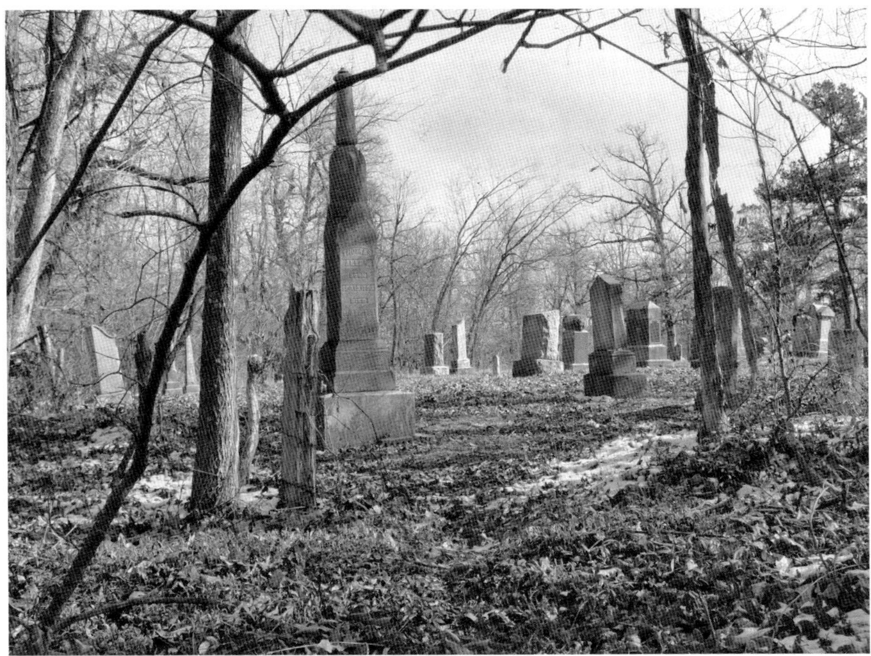

Spanish Fort Cemetery.

Builders were early Indians who fashioned burial mounds, fortifications and other earthworks found in the Middle West and Southeast. The Lawrence County ruins are much smaller than, but otherwise almost identical to, the immense Fort Ancient in Ohio, which was known to have been constructed by the Mound Builders as well. The Ohio site was four miles in circumference, compared to only a few hundred feet at Fort Ancient, but both were irregular circles with gateway openings and moats. As noted on the plaque, early Ozarks pioneers described the walls as about five feet high and the moat as two feet deep; however, it is believed that the original distance from the top of the wall to the bottom of the moat was at least fifteen feet.

Along with its ancient history, this location is the source of many tales that locals describe to be supernatural in origin, although during my visit to this location I experienced nothing paranormal. Many locals have reported hearing disembodied voices calling out to them, as well as hearing footsteps moving toward them with nothing visible to accompany them. Others have reported seeing what appear to be swirling balls of red light darting through the cemetery and into the trees just to disappear and then reappear again.

Several folks have taken photos of what appear to be black fog–like masses, as well as more solid-looking shadow people, and there have also been reports of what appears to be a grim reaper–like apparition moving about the graveyard and mound areas. Could these occurrences be the restless souls of former inhabitants of this location trying to make contact with the living, or are they just trying to scare the living into staying away? If you ever find yourself near Mount Vernon, Missouri, you could always stop off at the old Spanish Fort Cemetery and make that distinction yourself.

PEACE CHURCH CEMETERY

JOPLIN

If you ever find yourself traveling through Joplin, Missouri, you may want to stop off and ask a local where you might find Peace Church Cemetery. One of the oldest in Jasper County, it dates back to before the War Between the States. Peace Church, a Baptist church, was originally founded by the local community in 1855, and the cemetery was located on its grounds; it was quite common in those days for burial grounds to be on the same land as the church. The church was burned a long time ago, and all that remains today is the abandoned cemetery that belongs to no one but the people buried in it. The city will burn off the weeds after each winter, exposing the many headstones that normally cannot be seen other times of the year. The weeds will come back again strongly by the end of summer and can reach over six feet tall. There have been many attempts to clean up the cemetery, but it is usually forgotten about, as it would be very costly and take a lot of work just to clean it up and keep it maintained. On my first visit to Peace Church Cemetery, I was very shocked and saddened to see such a grand old cemetery forgotten in time to succumb to the elements and vandals. What is even more shocking to me is the fact that this cemetery is located in plain view on a very busy highway with thousands of people whizzing by in their vehicles every day, going about their lives, and they don't even give the place a second glance. Could one reason for the paranormal occurrences at Peace Church be due to all the souls interred there falling from human memory, with no connection to any living persons? While there I didn't have any sort of paranormal experiences, but a very heavy feeling of sadness was felt by myself and the others with me that day.

The cemetery was never platted so that no one would have to pay for a grave right. Because of this, burial records were not kept until after the Civil War. It is known that bodies have been buried on top of bodies due to this. Several events and stories bring people to this cemetery, one of which is the massacre at the nearby Rader Farm. The Battle of Carthage on July 5, 1861, was the beginning of a protracted four-year conflict that ended with hundreds of Jasper County residents dead and nearly all survivors forced to flee from the area. The Civil War in Jasper County began as civilly as war can be. Back then, armies had rules about how they fought and the preservation of civilian infrastructure, but the massacre at Rader Farm on May 18, 1863, changed all that.

According to plat maps from the time, the Rader farmhouse where the fighting took place was located about three hundred yards east of Peace Church Road and Fountain Road. Accounts of the action by Union and Confederate survivors show that soldiers on both sides crossed Peace Church Cemetery located nearby.

On May 18, 1863, Major Thomas Livingston was commander of a Rebel guerrilla unit of about seventy men that ambushed a Union foraging party that was collecting corn from the Rader Farm to feed soldiers at Fort Blair in Baxter Springs, Kansas. African American soldiers from Fort Blair, commanded by white soldiers of a Union artillery battery, were moving corn from the attic in the Rader Farm to wagons when Livingston's soldiers attacked from the woods as they came up from Peace Church Cemetery. The whole area was a field of chaos and bloodshed as U.S. soldiers scrambled desperately for their weapons, sought cover or simply tried to escape from the devastating surprise attack. Nearly half would be gunned down and their bodies mutilated, but some would escape and make their way all the way back that night to the Baxter Springs outpost, where they would tell their fellow comrades what had happened here.

The next morning, May 19, hundreds of Union soldiers from the Baxter camp showed up seeking retribution. Their commander, Colonel James Williams, was further enraged to find that the bodies of his ambushed troops had been severely mutilated. Because of the warm weather and this mutilation, the colonel decided perhaps it would be best to simply cremate the gory remains.

The corpses were placed in a ghastly pile in the Rader house, but before the flames were ignited, a Rebel prisoner who had apparently participated in the ambush the day before was brought before the colonel. The colonel had him marched into the house and shot dead and his body thrown on the

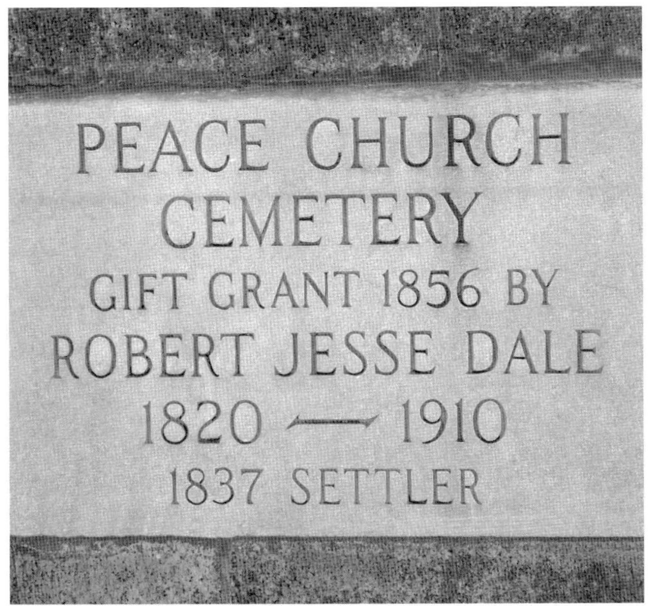

The gates of Peace Church Cemetery, Joplin, Missouri.

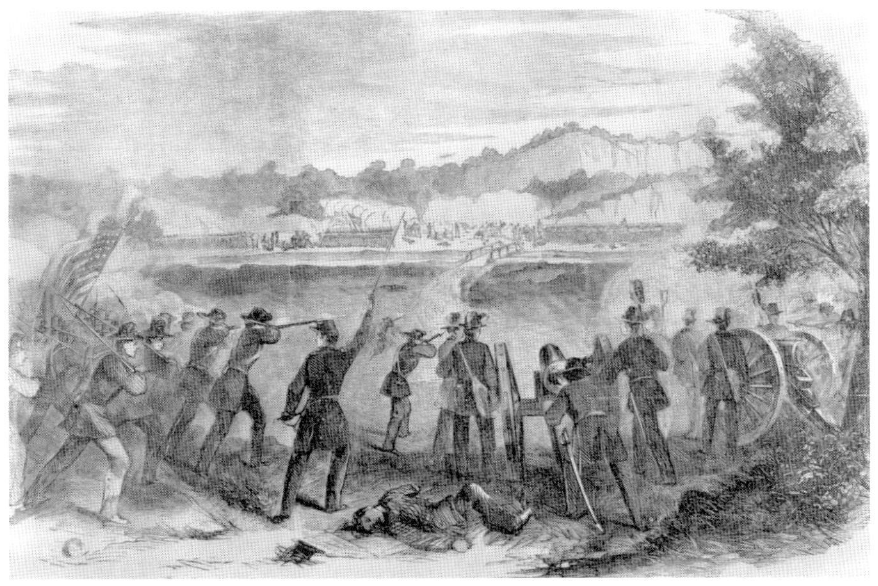

The Battle of Carthage near Peace Church Cemetery on May 18, 1863. *Courtesy of the Library of Congress.*

pile of mangled soldiers, and the structure was set ablaze, burning with the hot fury of the hell on Earth we call war. The massacre at the Rader Farm changed the tone of the conflict from somewhat civilized to something far more brutal. Over the years, many accounts of the apparitions of Civil War soldiers have been reported in the area of Peace Church Cemetery. Could these sightings be the lost souls of the victims of the gruesome conflict?

Tombstones stick like jagged stumps from the overgrown weeds of Peace Church Cemetery. An occasional plastic flower is placed on a grave, a colorful reminder that someone remembers the old, tree-lined cemetery. But the cemetery's most famous resident gets no flowers. Serial killer Billy Cook was buried under the anonymity of night in an unmarked grave at this cemetery and has since been hidden by history. Born in 1929 near Joplin, Missouri, spree killer William "Cockeyed" Cook, or Billy Cook as he is also known, was one of eight children fathered by an alcoholic miner. When his mother died, Cook's father moved the family into an abandoned Zink mine, where they lived like animals until the old man finally deserted them entirely. Welfare workers placed Cook's siblings in foster homes, but little William was repeatedly rejected due to a congenital deformity that prevented his right eye from closing completely. The resulting "sinister" look unnerved prospective foster parents, and Cook found placement only when the court agreed to pay his room and board. Unfortunately, Cook's appointed foster mother was more interested in earning money from the boy than raising him correctly. Two years running, Cook was given a bicycle for Christmas, and they were immediately repossessed for lack of payment. As he entered adolescence, he began to run the streets at night and practice petty theft. Upon his first arrest, he told the court he would prefer reform school to his foster home. Released a few months later, Cook immediately robbed a cab driver of eleven dollars, earning a five-year stretch in the reformatory. Violent outbursts there resulted in a transfer to the Old Missouri State Prison in Jefferson City, where he earned a reputation as a brawler. Once, Cook nearly killed a fellow inmate with a baseball bat, the incident resulting from a joke about his droopy eyelid.

Finally released from prison in 1950 at the age of twenty-two, Cook stopped in Joplin long enough for a reunion with his drunken father. He then drifted to the small desert town of Blythe, California, where he worked as a dishwasher until just before Christmas 1950. In late December, he headed east again. On the way he acquired a snub-nosed .32-caliber revolver in El Paso, Texas. He then doubled back east, wandering aimlessly across the country. The words "Hard Luck," tattooed across the fingers of his left hand, foretold the fate of hapless strangers who would cross his path. In Lubbock, Texas, on December 30, 1950, Cook abducted a motorist at gunpoint, pushing north toward Joplin. His hostage escaped in Oklahoma, and Cook ran out of gas on Highway 66, between Tulsa and Claremore, on New Year's Eve.

Carl Mosser, his wife and their three children were bound for New Mexico when they stopped to help another motorist in trouble. Their trip became a nightmare from the moment they laid eyes on William Cook. Flashing his pistol, Cook ordered Mosser to "drive him around." Stopping for gas and food in Wichita Falls, Texas, Mosser tried to disarm his captor, but Cook was quicker and stronger, firing several shots at a grocery clerk who tried to intervene. Over the next two days, Mosser drove Cook through New Mexico, Texas and Arkansas, winding up in the gunman's old stamping grounds around Joplin. There, Cook massacred the family (and their dog), dumping the bodies down an abandoned mine shaft before continuing his odyssey. His bloodstained car broke down in Osage County, Oklahoma, and Cook flagged down a deputy sheriff, disarming the officer, whom he left in a roadside ditch, his hands bound. Driving the stolen patrol car, Cook stopped a traveling salesman, Robert Dewey, and changed vehicles again, forcing Dewey to head for California. On arrival, Cook dispatched his hostage execution-style, the corpse and car alerting lawmen to his presence on the coast. Pushing south, Cook crossed the border at Tijuana, picking up two more male hostages en route. On January 15, 1951, he was recognized by the police chief in Santa Rosaria and disarmed without a struggle. Returned to California for trial on murder charges, Cook was sentenced to three hundred years in prison in 1951. According to a *Time* magazine article, the prosecutor left the courtroom shouting, "The God-Damndest travesty of justice, ever," because Cook had not been sentenced to death. Cook was later sentenced to death for the murder of the salesman. He was executed in San Quentin's gas chamber on December 12, 1952.

After twelve thousand people viewed Cook's body in Oklahoma, Cook was brought to Joplin. "Badman Bill Cook is buried at night in Peace Cemetery," read the headline of a 1952 *Joplin Globe* story by reporter Gerald Wallace.

The graveside service under the cover of darkness was officiated by Reverend Dow Booe of nearby Galena and lasted ten minutes. "Brief service held at night with aid of flashlights and lanterns before about 15 persons"; "Funeral cortege, consisting of four cars and hearse, moves to burial place over back roads," the sub-headlines read. "Just as the graveside rites ended," Wallace wrote, "the cry of a small child could be heard in

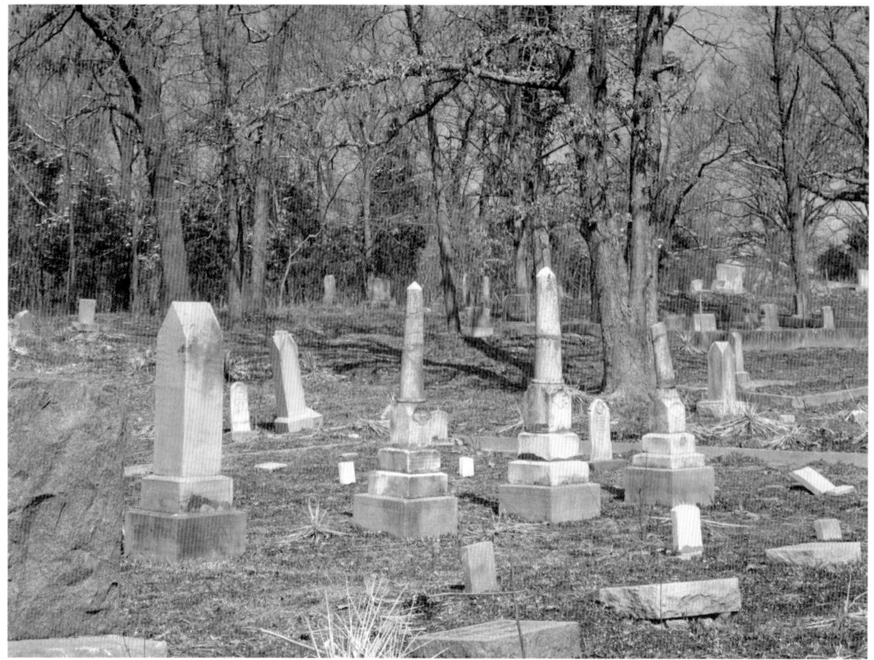

Peace Church Cemetery.

the chill of the night air." No one is really certain where the body of Cook is actually buried in the cemetery. Cook's body proved a nuisance to his relatives. With vandalism and several attempts of locals trying to dig him up, he was exhumed and buried in an unmarked grave in the right rear area of Peace Church Cemetery. There are some who claim Cook was buried outside Peace Church Cemetery at the request of locals who had family members buried there.

So, does Cook's lonely, pain-ridden ghost haunt Peace Church Cemetery? Today, Peace Church Cemetery is abandoned, but that doesn't stop the stories of the supernatural that abound in the area. Visitors have seen strange lights and heard disembodied voices at night, while others have seen what looks like a man standing in the woods watching them. Some have actually claimed that he was a real person until he quickly disappeared into nothingness. Many believe that the mysterious man is the ghost of Billy Cook trying to make it into the cemetery and finally find some peace. It's interesting that ghosts are associated as much with offenders as victims. Thus, our ghost story appears to feature an unrested soul among victims seeking peace or resolution.

Part II

Arkansas Ozarks

Yes, death. Death must be so beautiful. To lie in the soft brown earth, with the grasses waving above one's head, and listen to silence. To have no yesterday, and no tomorrow. To forget time, to forget life, to be at peace. You can help me. You can open for me the portals of death's house, for love is always with you, and love is stronger than death is.

—*Oscar Wilde,* The Canterville Ghost

CONFEDERATE CEMETERY

FAYETTEVILLE

The Fayetteville Confederate Cemetery situated along the gentle slope of an Ozarks ridge occupies a beautiful setting overlooking the historic northwest Arkansas city of Fayetteville. The cemetery contains the remains of men who fell in the service of the Confederacy in northwest Arkansas, primarily in Benton and Washington Counties. Some of the soldiers buried here died from illness in disease-ridden camps, while others fell in battle on one of the most violent and desperately contested fronts of the Civil War.

Their graves originally dotted the landscape of northwest Arkansas, but in 1878, the Southern Memorial Association of Washington County established the beautiful cemetery and exhumed fallen soldiers from throughout the region and brought them here for final burial. The effort coincided roughly with a similar effort to move Union dead in the region to Fayetteville National Cemetery.

Many of the soldiers buried at Confederate Cemetery fell in the Battle of Pea Ridge in March 1862 or at the Battle of Prairie Grove just nine months later. These two actions were among the fiercest of the Civil War in the West and firmly established Union control of the state of Missouri and northwest Arkansas. Brigadier General William Yarnell Slack, who died on March 20, 1862, from wounds received at Pea Ridge, is among the soldiers who now rest here. Others fell in the Battle of Fayetteville or numerous other smaller engagements fought throughout the region.

Many, however, died from sickness and disease during the brutal winters of 1861 and 1862, when Confederate soldiers in the Ozarks endured

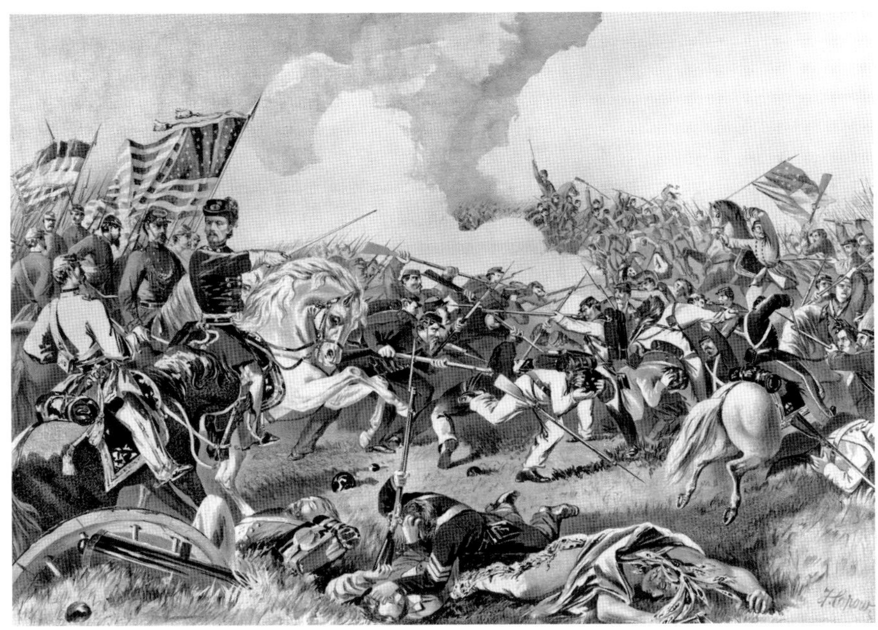

Battle of Pea Ridge near Fort Smith, Arkansas. *Courtesy of the Library of Congress.*

unimaginable privations. The cemetery contains hundreds of such graves, arrayed in beautiful rows beneath magnificent trees and commanding an outstanding view of the city of Fayetteville below. The rock wall surrounding the historic burial ground was built in 1885 of native stone. The tall Confederate monument on the grounds was erected around 1898 and forms a centerpiece of the cemetery.

Confederate Cemetery is located on Rock Street near the intersection of Willow on East Mountain just east of the downtown area. Many locals refer to East Mountain as "Ghost Mountain" due to the many legends revolving around it. Ghost Mountain overlooks a wooded hollow, which is the only untamed area in the main section of Fayetteville and overlooks the site of the Battle of Fayetteville.

The Confederate Cemetery is noted locally for strange anomalies showing up in photographs, and some people have claimed to see unusual lights along the ridge after dark. But these are not the only unexplained events witnessed in the area of the old cemetery. More famous in the area is the legend of the Burning Bride of Ghost Hollow.

Just across the street from the Confederate Cemetery is the Walker Cemetery, a small family plot. In this cemetery lies David Walker, the president

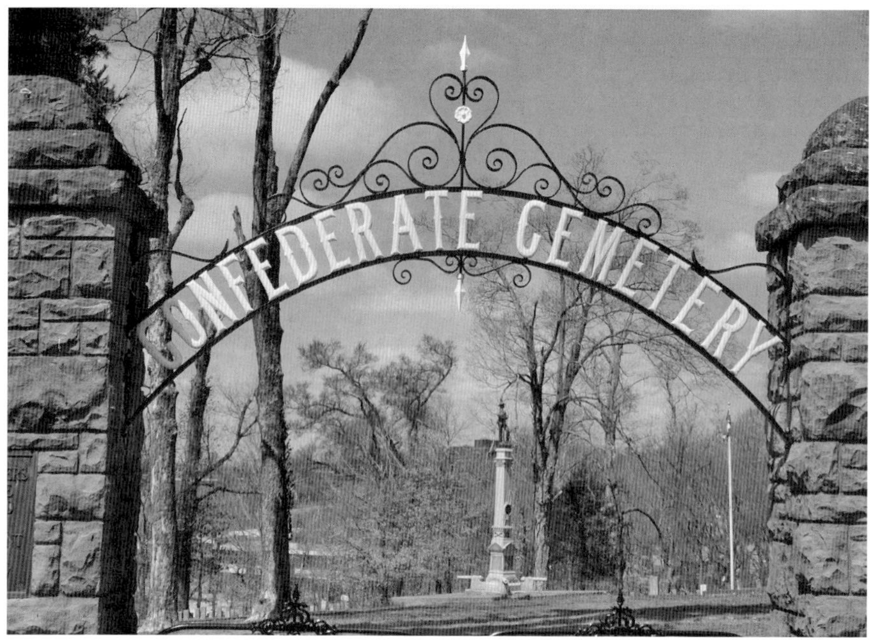

Confederate Cemetery, Fayetteville, Arkansas.

of the Secession Convention who was also Arkansas state senator, three times a state Supreme Court justice, one of the founders of the University of Arkansas and served as a colonel on the military board of General Sterling Price, plus other accomplishments in the field of law. He was married to Jane Lewis Washington, a third cousin of George Washington. His parents as well as his kinsmen are laid to rest there as well.

In 1872, Judge Walker had a two-story brick house constructed as a wedding present to his daughter and her new husband. The home still stands just next to the small family plot on East Mountain. As the years passed, it seemed the family couldn't keep any domestic help due to rumors of a horrible tragedy that had happened many years before on this same spot and had been circulating throughout the African American community. It seems that just after the Civil War had ended, a man and his young bride-to-be moved to Fayetteville from Fort Smith to get married and start a new life. They had constructed a home on the very spot where Judge Walker would later choose to build the two-story brick home on top of East Mountain. Legend has it that on her wedding night and without removing her wedding dress, the new bride leaned over the fireplace to stir the fire and a spark popped out onto her dress, setting it ablaze. Running and screaming hysterically, the new bride ran out the house and down into the hollow below, screaming to her death. From that day on, there have been reports from people who still see her apparition near both cemeteries and can hear her screams while she keeps reliving her tragic wedding night. It is also said that the Walker home is haunted by the ghost of Judge Walker, and he is often seen ascending the main stairwell in the old Georgian mansion.

Another source for the hauntings on Ghost Mountain could be due to another tale circulated in the Fayetteville area about a family who lived very near the Walker home back in the 1930s. Legend has it that the family lived in an old log house on top of the mountain. One night the husband came home very drunk, and his wife was caring for their sick child, who was crying incessantly. The man became so angry at the baby for keeping him awake that he jumped out of bed, grabbed the baby, stumbled outside and threw the baby down the well. The wife, of course, went into hysterics. She grabbed the well rope and jumped in to save her child. The drunken father took an axe and cut the rope, leaving his wife and child in the well. He left town, never to be seen again. The source of these legends may be based more on myth than fact, but one thing is for sure—the legends of "Ghost Mountain" remain a source of fear for many living in the Fayetteville area to this day.

FORT SMITH NATIONAL CEMETERY

FORT SMITH

Fort Smith National Cemetery is located in Sebastian County, Arkansas. Fort Smith has played an important role in the expansion and development of the United States. By the early nineteenth century, more and more white settlers were moving into the territory acquired through the Louisiana Purchase of 1805. Tensions with the local Native Americans increased as both groups competed for space and resources. To ensure the safety of the settlers, the U.S. Army established a string of military posts along the western frontier. Fort Smith was the first and westernmost of these. This rough and rowdy border town was the jumping-off place into Indian Territory for outlaws, bandits and renegades.

On Christmas Day 1817, General William Bradford and his men arrived on the point of land just below the confluence of the Poteau and Arkansas Rivers, where they began constructing a stockade fort sufficient for one company. Within a few years of its establishment, additional troops were garrisoned to maintain peace and prevent hostilities between the Cherokee and the Osage. However, fifty men (about 25 percent of the command) died in 1823, with forty-four of the deaths occurring during the summer months. Despite its strategic importance, the army closed the fort in 1824. Doors, windows and all other movable equipment at Fort Smith were transported to Fort Gibson for use in the construction of that post.

The first cemetery at Fort Smith was most likely established during this period. A newspaper article published in 1841 suggests there was a dilapidated burial ground outside the stockade containing three graves marked by marble slabs. This cemetery may have been established in 1819 at the time of, or just prior to, the death of the Fort Smith surgeon Thomas Russell.

In 1838, the army permanently returned to Fort Smith with the arrival of Company F, Seventh U.S. Infantry. A new garrison was constructed, including an officers' log house, where General Zachary Taylor lived from 1841 until 1845. In addition, the original post cemetery was rehabilitated and enlarged. On April 23, 1861, at the onset of the Civil War, Fort Smith was evacuated and Confederate forces occupied the garrison. By May of that year, the Arkansas legislature had ceded the fort to the Confederate States of America. During the War Between the States, more than four hundred Confederate soldiers were buried at Fort Smith, including Generals James B. McIntosh and Alexander E. Steen. On September 1, 1863, Union troops were able to retake Fort Smith, and it remained in Union hands for the rest of the war.

In 1867, the old post burial ground was elevated to a national cemetery consisting of about five acres enclosed by a whitewashed fence. Many military dead were removed from battlefields and private cemeteries and reinterred here—so many, in fact, that when the Fort Smith military reservation closed in 1871, President Grant ordered that Fort Smith National Cemetery be reactivated by the War Department and remain open for the purpose of future military burials.

Probably the most famous interment at Fort Smith is Isaac C. Parker, better known as the "Hanging Judge." Parker was born in 1838 in Ohio and began practicing law in 1859; during the Civil War, he was a corporal assigned to the Sixty-first Missouri Infantry. After the war, Parker became a judge for the Twelfth Circuit of Missouri and was elected to Congress twice. In 1875, President Grant appointed him U.S. district judge for the Western District of Arkansas. At the relatively young age of thirty-seven, Parker found himself responsible for a seventy-four-thousand-square-mile area. In a territory noted for its lawlessness, his harsh but effective administration helped make the settlement of the West possible. On November 17, 1896, two months after Judge Parker was removed from office due to a movement toward the establishment of local courts, he died and was buried at Fort Smith National Cemetery.

Also buried at this cemetery is Fort Smith native Brigadier General William O. Darby, who organized and commanded the First Ranger Battalion, or "Darby's Rangers." The highly decorated Colonel Darby was killed in Italy's

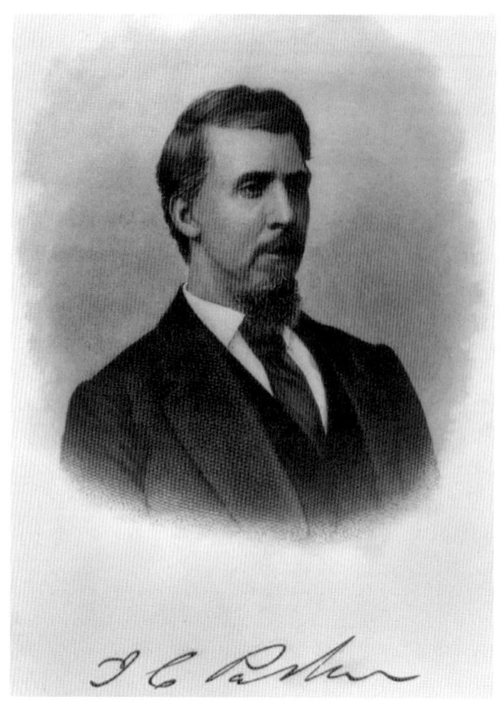

Left: Judge Isaac Parker (the "Hanging Judge") of Fort Smith. *Courtesy of the Library of Congress.*

Below: Fort Smith National Cemetery, Fort Smith, Arkansas.

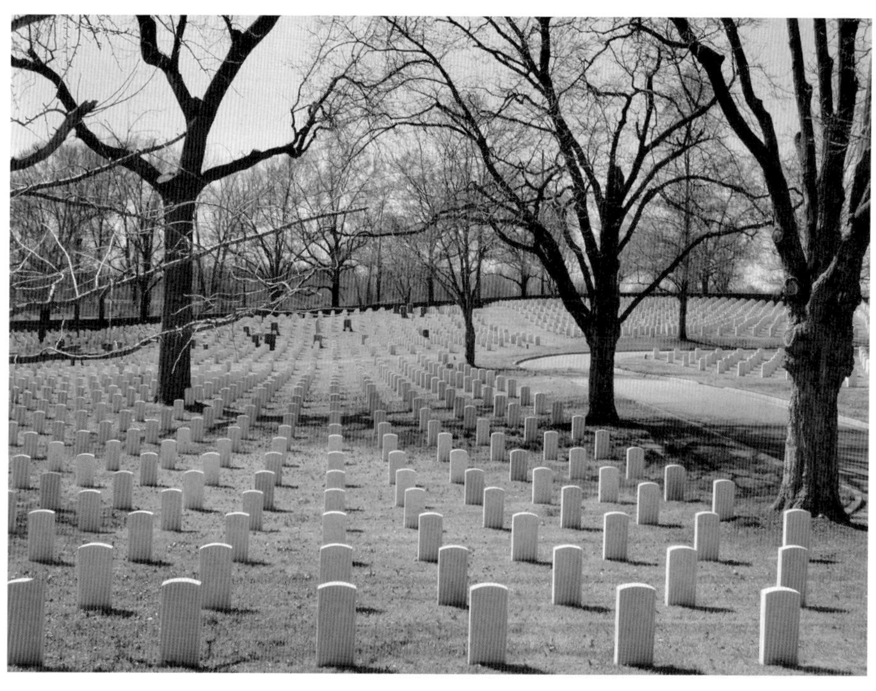

Po Valley only days before the end of World War II; he was posthumously promoted to the rank of brigadier general.

The once-small cemetery at Fort Smith has been expanded several times over almost two hundred years and today totals thirty-two acres. Many of the private monuments in the national cemetery face west, in the opposite direction of government-furnished headstones. This is in accordance with a religious custom in some Arkansas communities to bury the dead with the feet to the east so that on Resurrection Day the body will arise facing east. The inscription is facing west, as it is believed that a person, when reading the headstone, would be in a proper position (facing east) to say a prayer for the deceased. Fort Smith National Cemetery was placed on the National Register of Historic Places on May 29, 1999.

Though Fort Smith's most famous judge Isaac C. Parker died in 1896, he remains an active figure among the paranormal community. During his twenty-one years on the federal bench, Parker sentenced 160 people to death by hanging, with 79 of those people ultimately receiving the punishment. With such a vibrant past surrounding death, it's no surprise Parker has become home to several paranormal legends in Fort Smith.

His job is better remembered than his name. Isaac Parker was the U.S. district judge for the Western District of Arkansas, but in Old West legend as well as modern movies, he was the "Hanging Judge" of Fort Smith. During his career, more than seventy men found guilty in Parker's courtroom were executed on the gallows at Fort Smith. Contrary to legend, however, the executions were generally carried out away from public view, and there is no evidence that Parker himself ever watched any of them.

It may be surprising to learn that the man remembered as the "Hanging Judge" was actually opposed to capital punishment. But in many of the cases tried before him, there was no other sentence he could have handed down. Federal law then required that persons convicted of rape or murder be executed. Hanging Judge Parker, however, did not approve and urged that the laws be changed. He argued that capital punishment was not a deterrent to crime.

Parker and his marshals became well known in western lore because they had the responsibility of patrolling not just western Arkansas but the frontier as well. Parker was responsible for enforcing U.S. law in the Indian Nations of Oklahoma, where many outlaws had assembled under the mistaken belief that they would be safe from capture. They preyed heavily on the peaceful people living in the Nations, as well as on travelers in the region. Assisted by Native American tribal police, Parker's team of deputy U.S. marshals brought justice to the frontier.

Although most of the judge's deputy marshals were white, he was unique for his time in that he also employed deputies who were of African American and Native American descent. The suspects they arrested, likewise, represented a variety of races.

Among the more infamous outlaws to spend time at Fort Smith's notorious "Hell on the Border" jail were Belle Starr, "Cherokee" Bill and members of the Rufus Buck Gang and the Dalton Gang. Modern movies based on the efforts to apprehend such men (and women) include Clint Eastwood's *Hang 'Em High*, along with *True Grit* and *Rooster Cogburn*. Being a deputy marshal for Judge Parker was even more dangerous than portrayed in the movies. Sixty-five of his officers died in the line of duty. One who survived was Cal Whitson, the "real" Rooster Cogburn.

Located in the basement of the old Fort Smith barracks was the "Hell on the Border" jail, where inmates awaited trial or execution. Conditions were horrible, and Judge Parker and a number of others lobbied for a more decent facility, which Congress finally authorized in 1886. The new jail, which still stands, was constructed as a wing on the original barracks building.

Perhaps the most frightening tale to come out of the cemetery comes from a groundskeeper at the Fort Smith National Cemetery, where Parker and his wife are now buried. On a cold December night in 1998, a groundskeeper

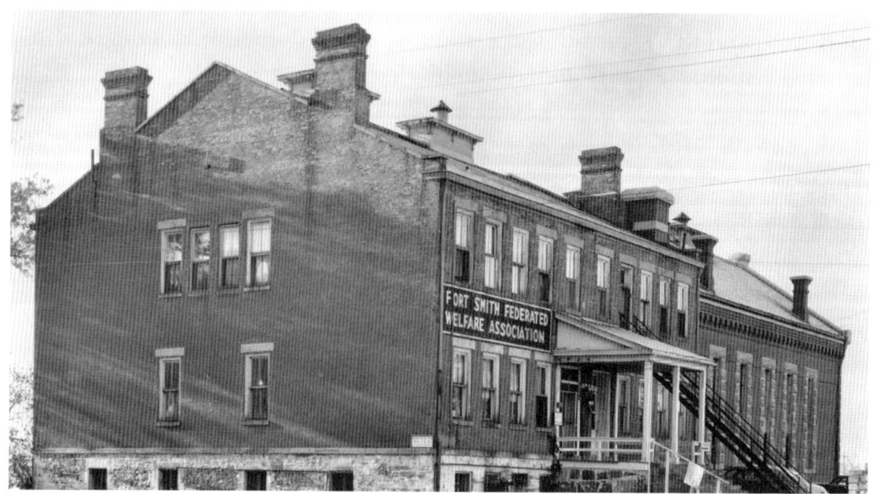

The old courthouse, Fort Smith, Arkansas. *Courtesy of the Library of Congress.*

had an experience that left him shaken to the core. He was on his way to retrieve some tools as dusk approached when he heard a strange noise that kept repeating. As it approached, he realized the noise was footsteps crunching in the crisp winter grass.

The groundskeeper reported he felt like he was being followed. After retrieving his tools, he turned on a flashlight and turned around, and in the beam of his flashlight, there was an old man. The man stood there looking back at him. The groundskeeper realized he could see through the man who stood before him with white hair and a white beard, wearing an old black suit. He then asked the old man what he wanted, at which time he started to move his mouth with no sound coming from his lips. Needless to say, the groundskeeper took off, dropping the flashlight and speeding away in his car. The groundskeeper distinctly described the old man as Judge Parker based on the images he had seen of him during his many trips to the Fort Smith Museum. Judge Parker's vibrant courtroom history has made him into one of Fort Smith's top haunting legends. Chilling tales involving the "Hanging Judge" are likely to continue to be told for many years to come.

Possum Walk Cemetery

Coal Hill

Near the very small town of Coal Hill lies what is thought to be one of the oldest cemeteries in the state of Arkansas. Possum Walk Cemetery is located just past the western side of Coal Hill. Out of the several hundred known grave sites here, only about thirty-four are fitted with inscribed tombstones. Most graves in the cemetery just have small rocks placed on them to mark where a long-forgotten soul is buried. Most of the people buried at Possum Walk were very poor, with most of them being African Americans and convicts who perished in the local coal mines. The last known burial at the site is that of a Hatfield who died in 1912.

The town of Coal Hill is on U.S. Highway 64, in the western end of Johnson County. Coal Hill lies five miles north of the Arkansas River in gently rolling hills to the north of the river valley. It was incorporated on January 8, 1880. It originally was called Whalen's Switch, then Eureka and finally Coal Hill. The town was named by Mose Butts, an early official, after the coal beneath the ground and the hills rising above the little city. In 1912, Coal Hill was the largest town in Johnson County.

Just as coal is the reason for the town's name, it is the reason for its growth and demise. In 1840, coal was discovered on the east bank of Spadra Creek, east of Coal Hill. This was reportedly the first anthracite coal discovery west of the Mississippi River. However, due to the difficulty of mining and transporting the coal, it was not mined to any advantage for several years. In 1872, the Little Rock and Fort Smith Railroad reached Clarksville, opening eastern Johnson County coal fields for exploration. As railroad connections

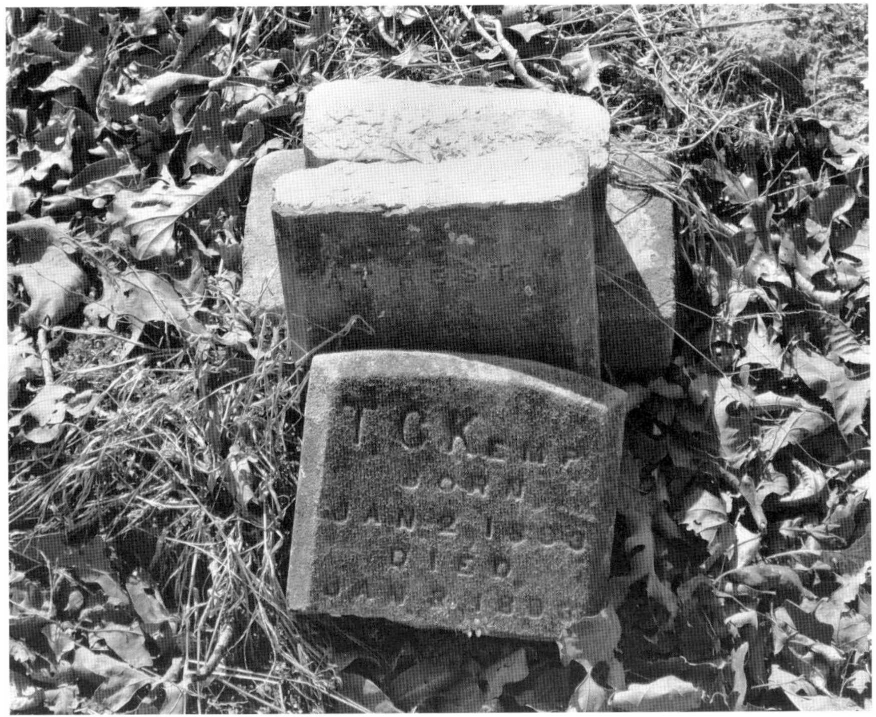

Possum Walk Cemetery near Coal Hill, Arkansas.

grew in the late 1870s, the mining industry began a real boom, as both miners and company men began to flood into Johnson County. In 1888, it became the center of a state investigation into the mistreatment of convict labor employed in the mines. The investigation helped lead to the abolition of the much-abused system.

Much of the labor for the mines was provided by African Americans who lived in a segregated community on the west side of town near Possum Walk Cemetery. More than two hundred black citizens lived in the community in 1890. Additional labor was provided by convicts from the convict lease system.

Coal Hill continued to prosper until a decline in the county coal mining industry by the early 1920s. During that time, there were twenty-three county coal mines in operation. By the mid-1930s, the number had declined to just eight. Though Coal Hill was the second-largest Johnson County town in the 1920s and 1930s, people began to move away to seek employment elsewhere. By 1960, the population of 704 stood as its twentieth-century low.

Many of the present-day residents of Coal Hill feel that there are more than a few of the town's past residents who are still among them—but in spirit only. Many visitors to Possum Walk Cemetery have reported feeling a horrible chill going through them even on the hottest summer nights, and many others have seen dark shadow-like forms that follow them around the cemetery. It is told that when you walk into the graveyard, you can hear somebody walking behind you when no one is actually there. Many people report hearing whispering and grunting in their ears. If you are lucky, you can catch a glimpse out of the corner of your eye of someone standing there looking straight at you, but when you turn to see who it is, there is no one there. Many locals say that the spirit that looks at you is that of a woman who died during childbirth searching for her baby. It seems probable that more than one of the hauntings of Possum Walk Cemetery can be attributed to the many poor souls who perished in the mines of Coal Hill. Could it be they are looking for some sort of absolution for the atrocities that were placed on them by the mining companies and those who they feel are responsible for their demise?

Mount Holly Cemetery

Little Rock

Located in Little Rock, Arkansas, at the southernmost edge of the Ozarks Plateau, Mount Holly Cemetery is often called the Westminster Abbey of Arkansas, a name that seems justified by the great number of individuals of significance in the fields of art, literature, religion, war and politics who are buried there. Eleven Arkansas governors are interred therein, as well as thirteen state Supreme Court justices, four United States senators, four Confederate generals, twenty-one Little Rock mayors, an Indian princess and a boy martyr.

Mount Holly Cemetery dates from February 23, 1843, when ground was deeded by two leading citizens, Chester Ashley and Roswell Beebe, to the City of Little Rock. The cemetery is located on a four-square-block site between Eleventh and Thirteenth Streets and from Broadway to Gaines Street. The cemetery remains its original twenty-acre size. Before the establishment of Mount Holly, burials were made in private family cemeteries and a public burial ground on what would first become the Peabody School site and later the location of the present-day Federal Building at Capitol Avenue and Gaines Street. A number of grave markers with dates predating the formation of Mount Holly represent reinterments from the Capitol Avenue site.

Feeling the town fathers were not giving the cemetery the attention it deserved, a group of Little Rock businessmen formed a cemetery commission on March 20, 1877. Charter members of the commission were J.H. Haney, Fay Hempstead, James Austin Henry, Philo O. Hooper

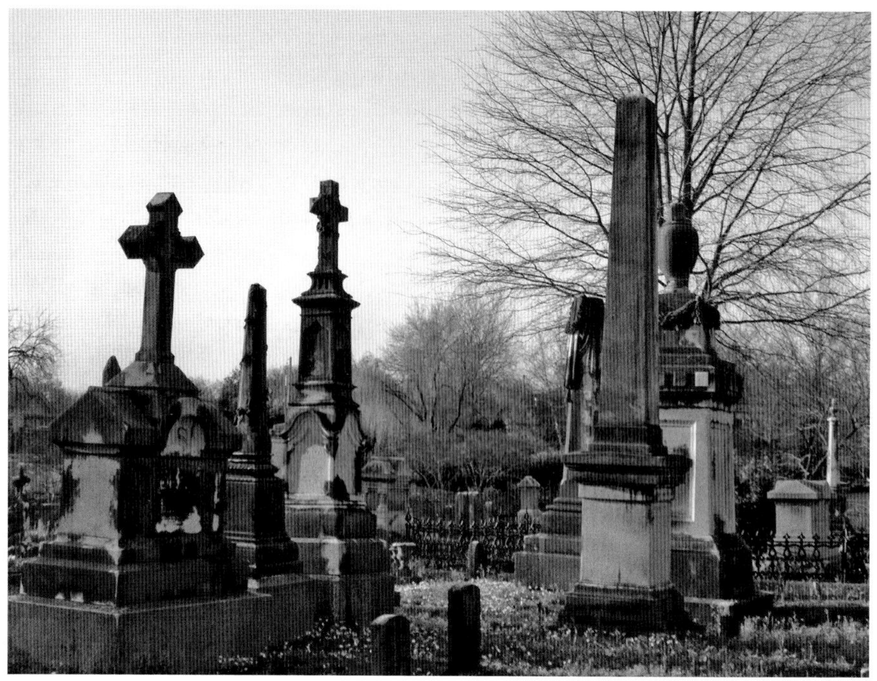

Various grave sites at Mount Holly Cemetery, Little Rock, Arkansas.

and Frederick Kramer. This form of cemetery administration continued for almost forty years until a contingent of the town's women became critical of the cemetery's unkempt appearance and took over the reins from the men. Following adoption of City Ordinance No. 2199 in June 1915, the ladies' Mount Holly Cemetery Association was incorporated on July 20, 1915; it continues in that role.

A national study made in 1940 indicated that Arkansas had fewer foreign-born residents than any other state in the union. This demographic statistic is borne out by the cemetery's burial index, which indicates that most of the early deceased were native-born. On March 7, 1843, a city ordinance designated a portion of the cemetery for Catholic burials, but with the formal opening of Little Rock's Calvary Cemetery on Asher Avenue in 1872, most Catholic burials were thereafter made there. Between 1860 and 1862, early members of Little Rock's Jewish community made use of twelve lots purchased exclusively for their use. Many of these remains were removed to Oakland Cemetery (on Little Rock's east side) between 1913 and 1916, when its Jewish section became available. Section 9 of a March 7, 1843 city ordinance called for a portion of Lot No. 210 at Mount Holly to be set aside for the interment of African Americans, described in the ordinance as "deceased persons of color."

As befits its City of Roses location, the cemetery's many varieties of old roses, mature trees, handcrafted signs that identify its narrow lanes and styles of its structures give Mount Holly a look of understated Victorian elegance. Its Victorian ambience is further reflected in its grave markers, which exhibit interesting iconographic motifs and epitaphic material and include a number of white bronze markers (manufactured only between 1875 and 1915). Several grave markers are the work of mainstream American stone carvers, and the marker for Albert Pike's family (which Pike designed) is the work of Robert Eberhard Launitz, said to be the father of monumental art in America. Mount Holly's collection of cemetery furniture includes a number of very old cast-iron pieces, and ornate iron fencing encloses several older lots. A handsome cast-iron fountain, a nineteenth-century product of the famous J.L. Mott Company of Bronx, New York, has been at the cemetery since 2002. With cremation's growing popularity, both locally and nationally, a columbarium was completed in 2003 to the west of the handsomely landscaped fountain.

In 1884, 640 Confederate soldiers buried in Mount Holly (troops belonging to commands from Missouri, Arkansas, Texas and Louisiana) were removed to Oakland Cemetery, with a monument erected there in their honor by trustees of the Mount Holly Cemetery Commission. Structures within the cemetery offer a wide range of architectural styles and include private mausoleums, a community mausoleum, a sexton's cottage, a picturesque Carpenter Gothic bell house and a receiving house dating back to 1897, which was restored in 1996. The community mausoleum, designed by Charles L. Thompson, a noted Little Rock architect, is reminiscent of the style of John Russell Pope, architect of the National Archives in Washington, and typical of the period from 1915 to 1925.

For those interested in ghostly happenings and the paranormal, you will have more than your fill at Mount Holly Cemetery. The dead don't appear to be completely at rest in Mount Holly Cemetery, as it is rumored to be a hotbed of paranormal activity. Visitors to the cemetery have reported statues that move in front of startled visitors and sometimes even mysteriously show up on the lawns of the houses located near the cemetery. People have reported seeing human-like apparitions both at night as well as during the day, and some have taken photos at the cemetery that have ghostly images of apparitions dressed in period clothing and strange lights and mists in them.

Many have reported hearing a ghostly flute echoing from nowhere in the cemetery. People who live around the cemetery have reported finding pieces of graves or statues placed mysteriously on their lawns, and it's also reported that trinkets mysteriously appear and disappear on graves.

Although not a governor, general or wealthy citizen, the most notable person interred at Mount Holly and the source of speculation into some of the paranormal activity in the cemetery is David Owen Dodd, known after his death as the "Boy Martyr of the Confederacy." Over the years, there have been many sightings of an apparition of what people believe to be the tormented spirit of Dodd wandering the cemetery, possibly seeking resolution for his unjust hanging at the hands of Union troops on January 8, 1864.

David Owen Dodd was born on November 10, 1846, in Victoria, Lavaca County, Texas, to Andrew Marion Dodd, a merchant, and Lydia Echols Owen. His Baptist parents had married in a village south of Little Rock, Arkansas, and moved with daughter Senorah to Texas, where David and his sisters, Leonora and Ann Eliza, were born. David's third sister, Ann Eliza, died before the Civil War.

In 1856, the family returned to Arkansas and settled near Benton. In 1861, the Dodds moved to Little Rock to be closer to Senorah, who attended school in the city and lived with her aunt, Mrs. Susan A. Dodd. David Dodd went to classes at St. John's Masonic College. His father left the family to serve as sutler with the Third Arkansas Cavalry. In 1862, David went to Louisiana and worked as a telegraph operator before crossing the river to join his father and assist him in his sutlery. In the fall of 1863, after the Union army occupied Little Rock, David returned to escort his mother and sisters to Mississippi but never left Arkansas. In December, his father arrived, and the entire Dodd family moved south to journey to Mississippi to be near Andrew.

As Union troops destroyed Southern fields, tobacco was becoming scarce. Andrew Dodd devised a plan to buy tobacco and store it for later sale at a higher price. He looked to his business associates in Little Rock for the needed cash. Because Little Rock was in Union hands, he could not make the trip himself. On December 24, 1863, he sent David Dodd, a minor and therefore assumed neutral, to Little Rock to deliver letters to former associates seeking investments for the tobacco deal. Confederate general James F. Fagan issued the boy a pass. Dodd rode a mule to Little Rock, carrying a birth certificate showing he was an underage seventeen along with his pass.

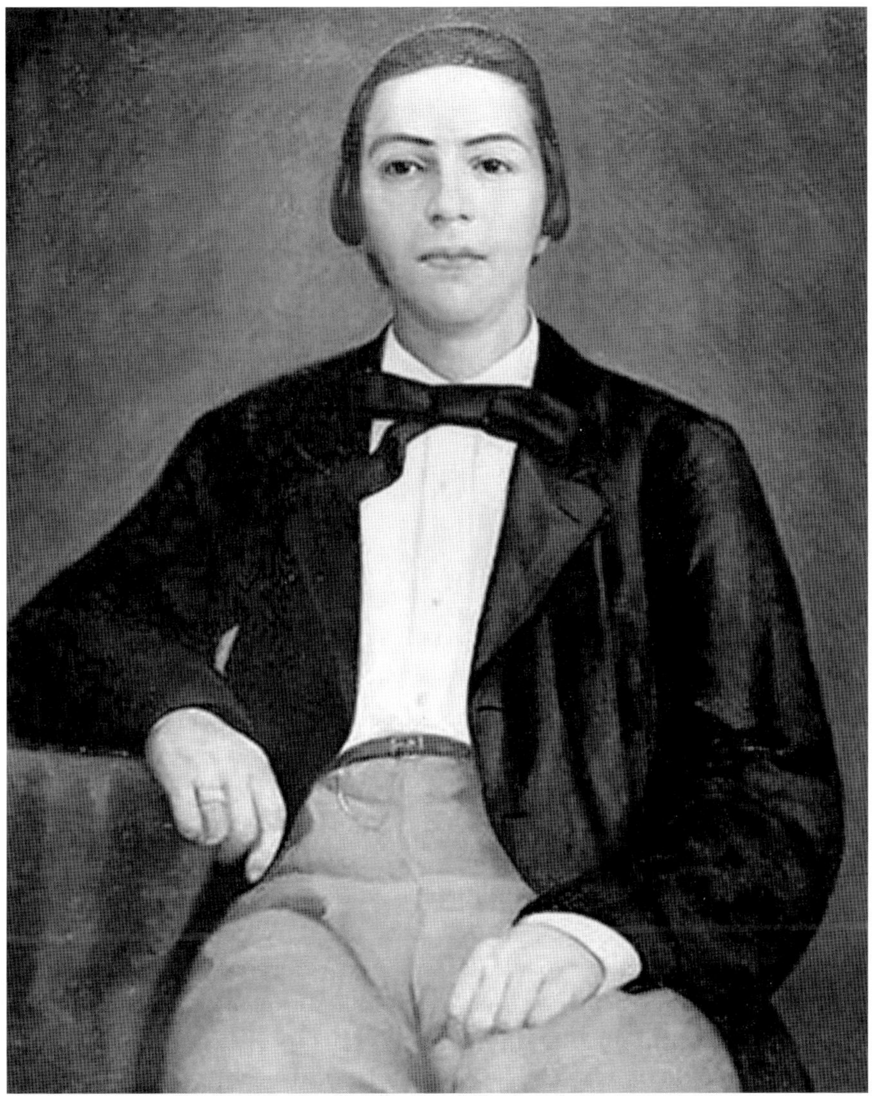

A portrait of David O. Dodd, age seventeen, Little Rock, Arkansas. *Courtesy of the Library of Congress.*

Dodd stayed with his aunt, Mrs. Susan Dodd, in Little Rock. Except for some Union soldiers, there were very few teenage boys in the city, and Dodd was popular with the city's younger girls. He even became popular with some of the younger servicemen at the arsenal, especially because he usually was accompanied by a local girl or two. In addition to his father's letters, he also delivered letters to several people he knew. Dodd attended some holiday dances with at least two girls, Mary Swindle and Minerva Cogburn. He also spent some time with sixteen-year-old Mary Dodge at her home, where Union officers were quartered. Mary supported the Southern cause; her father, R.L. Dodge, was a Vermont native on friendly terms with the Northern troops.

On December 28, 1863, Dodd visited the provost marshal's office at St. John's College (several hundred yards southwest of the arsenal) and had no trouble obtaining a pass through Union lines to rejoin his family in Camden. Dodd left Little Rock the next day. As he left Union territory, the guard tore up Dodd's pass since he would no longer need it now that he was in Confederate land. He went to spend the night with his uncle, Washington Dodd, on the Middle Hot Springs Road southwest of Little Rock. The next day, Dodd traveled through the woods and found himself back behind Union lines.

On December 29, 1863, Dodd was stopped by a Union sentry in west Little Rock, near Ten Mile House on Stagecoach Road, and was discovered to be without a pass. For identification, he showed his small leather notebook, where Union soldiers found his birth certificate and a page with dots and dashes. A Union officer was able to read some of the Morse code messages, which contained information about Union troop strength and locations in Little Rock. Dodd was arrested on the spot.

The next day, Dodd was taken to Little Rock to face Brigadier General John Davidson, who was commanding the Union occupation forces in General Frederick Steele's absence. A telegraph operator translated the Morse code, which provided precise locations and strengths of Union troops. David was formally charged as a spy and taken to the military prison on the site of the present Arkansas State Capitol building. Dodd was interrogated for two days by Union officers, who tried to discover the source of the information. On the third day, under personal orders from General Steele, Mary Dodge and her father were escorted under armed guard to a Union gunboat on the Arkansas River and transported to Vermont, where Mary was kept until the end of the war. This suggests that Steele had discovered that Mary Dodge was involved and that he would not be able to hang a sixteen-year-old girl.

On December 31, 1863, Dodd's trial began in Little Rock by a military tribunal of six Union officers. Brigadier General John M. Thayer presided, with Captain B.F. Rice as judge advocate. Other members were Colonel John A. Garrett, Major Phineas Graves, Major H.D. Gibson and Captain

George Rockwell. The court-martial lasted four days. The official charges were read by the judge advocate:

> *In this, that said David O. Dodd, an inhabitant of the State of Arkansas, did as a Spy of the so-called Confederate States of America, enter within the lines of the Army of the United States, stationed at Little Rock, Arkansas, and did there secretly possess himself of information regarding the number, the kind, and position of the troops of said Army of the United States, their commanders, and other military information valuable to the enemy now at war with the United States, and having thus obtained said information did obtain a pass from the Provost Marshal General's office, and endeavor to reach the lines of the enemy—therewith; when he was arrested at the cavalry outposts of said Army—and did otherwise lurk, and act as a spy of the Rebels now in arms against the United States—This at the Post of Little Rock, and the encampments of the Army of Arkansas, on or about the 29th and 30th of December, 1863.*

To these charges, David pleaded not guilty.

On January 1, 1864, the trial continued with Dodd represented by attorneys T.D.W. Yonley and William Fishback, who was pro-Union and later became governor of Arkansas. The defense attorneys proposed amnesty, which was rejected by the tribunal after an adjournment to deliberate the matter. Court was adjourned until the next day.

On January 2, 1864, witnesses were called to testify against Dodd. Private Daniel Goldberg testified that he had torn up Dodd's pass because "he did not need a pass anymore." Sergeant Frederick Miehr testified that he arrested Dodd after the boy could not produce a pass. First Lieutenant C.F. Stopral found Dodd's memoranda book, discovered that the Morse code reported the positions and armaments of the Third Ohio Battery and Eleventh Ohio Battery and sent him to the guardhouse. Captain George Hanna testified that he interrogated Dodd and discovered that Dodd was carrying one pocketbook containing Louisiana money, Confederate money, ten dollars in greenbacks and some Confederate postage stamps; one postal currency holder; one loaded Derringer pistol; and a package between his shirts containing letters. Captain John Baird testified that, per Hanna's orders, he took the prisoner and the papers into Little Rock the next morning to General Davidson. Captain Robert C. Clowery testified that he interpreted the Morse code as containing detailed information about the locations and strengths of Union forces and armaments. First Lieutenant George O.

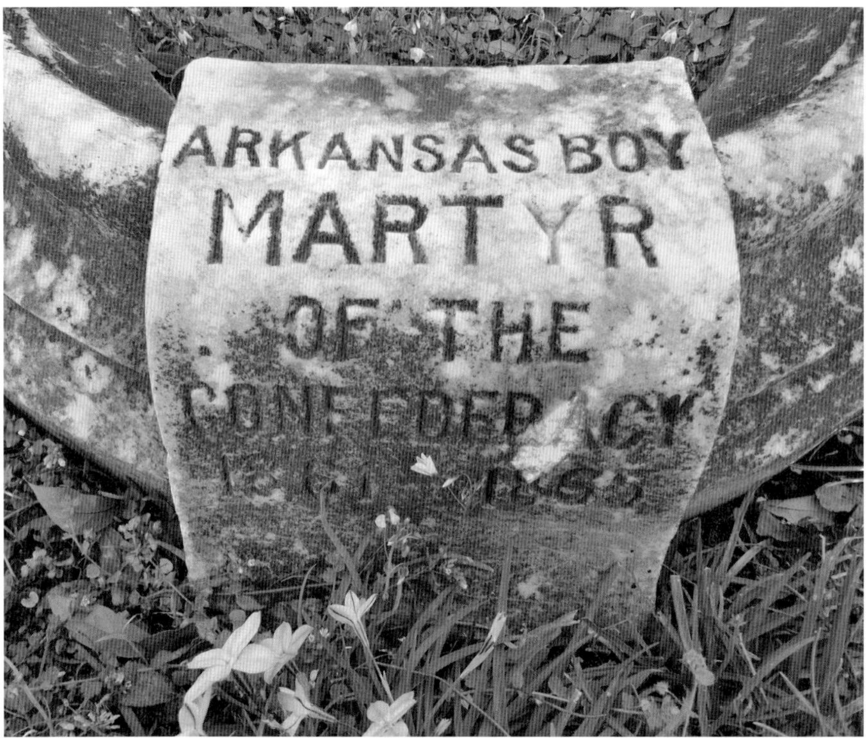

The grave of Dodd, Mount Holly Cemetery, Little Rock, Arkansas.

Sokalski then testified about the actual Union troop strength and weaponry, which were matches of Dodd's coded message.

During the trial, Dodd was asked several times to name the Union traitor who gave him the troop information; each time he remained silent. The defense tried to explain the Morse code information as something Dodd did to exercise his telegraph skills. Dodd did not testify, although his written deposition was submitted. Only character witnesses were called.

By a 4–2 vote, David Dodd was convicted of spying for the Confederacy and was sentenced to be hanged. He was taken back to the state prison. General Steele designated Friday, January 8, 1864, for the execution day.

On January 8, David O. Dodd was brought to the grounds of his former school, St. John's, just east of the Little Rock Arsenal, for his hanging. A crowd of five or six thousand gathered to watch the hanging. Dodd stood on the tailgate of a wagon under the noose. The executioner, named Dekay, fixed the rope around David's neck, and the prop was knocked from under the tailgate. The rope stretched and the boy dangled, strangling to death over a full five minutes. It is said that onlookers and Union soldiers became ill at the sight of this.

The record is unclear about exactly how Dodd died. Some contend that one or two soldiers grabbed his legs to add weight and hasten his death. Others told that a soldier shinnied up the gibbet to grab the noose, twist the rope and raise the condemned off the ground. Military doctors who examined Dodd's body reported death due to "a disrupted spine."

Just prior to the funeral, Union headquarters ordered no spoken or sung words at the memorial service and stated that only Dodd's relatives in Union-held territory (two aunts and their husbands) would be allowed to attend. The town was tense; a riot was possible, and there was fear that a Confederate raid would take advantage of the situation. Security around General Steele's headquarters was increased; no one was allowed to see him except on official business. Calm prevailed, and David O. Dodd was buried

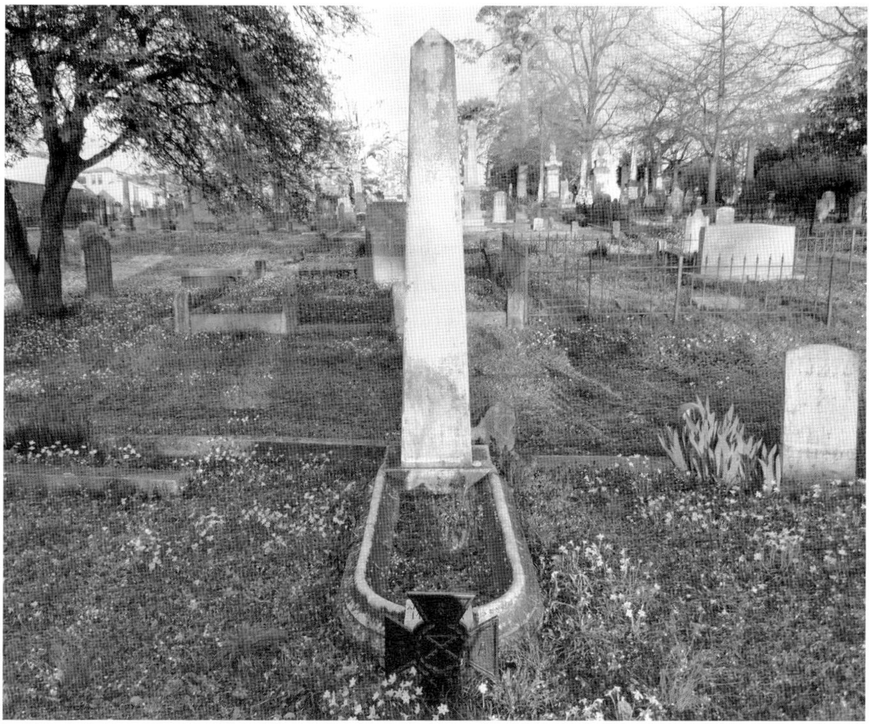

Dodd's grave. *Courtesy of Shane Wade Corkren.*

in plot Elm 355 in the southeast portion of Mount Holly Cemetery in Little Rock, in a grave donated by a Little Rock resident.

At a time when Union sympathies ran high in Arkansas and a constitutional convention was in session to enable the state to rejoin the Union, Dodd's execution fueled renewed divisions between Union and Confederate factions. Dodd quickly became a folk hero and a force behind renewed Confederate dissension. After hearing the news of their son's execution, Andrew and Lydia Dodd spent the remainder of their lives in ill health. Andrew died of yellow fever in 1867, while Lydia died in Pascagoula, Mississippi, in 1885.

To date, Mount Holly Cemetery is the most beautifully ornate cemetery that I have had the pleasure of visiting with the exception of Highgate Cemetery in North London, England. Whether you're out looking for a dose of history or hoping to catch a glimpse of spirits past, Mount Holly will surely not disappoint.

White County Fairgrounds, "Poor Farm Cemetery"

Searcy

The White County "Paupers' Farm" of the late 1800s and early 1900s consisted of 120 acres where the White County Fairgrounds are now located in Searcy, Arkansas. Often the poorhouse was situated on the grounds of a poor farm on which able-bodied residents were required to work. Such farms were common in the United States in the nineteenth and early twentieth centuries; it could even be part of the same economic complex as a prison farm and other penal or charitable public institutions. Poor farms were county- or town-run residences where paupers (mainly elderly and disabled people) were supported at public expense. They were common in the United States beginning in the middle of the nineteenth century and declined in use after the Social Security Act took effect in 1935, with most disappearing completely by about 1950.

The people who died at the White County Paupers' Farm were buried in a cemetery that was located where the livestock display building is now at the fairgrounds. The cemetery was called the County Farm Cemetery. It is known that there are more than one hundred mostly unmarked graves in the cemetery. At the county farm, the dead were placed in plain wooden caskets in graves often dug by fellow residents. The earlier markers were probably wood slats, though later graves featured concrete slabs adorned with nothing but a number—no names, dates of birth and death or epitaphs. According to one fairground employee to whom we spoke during our visit to the site, "There were two graves with tombstones still on the site when this part of the poorhouse cemetery was being incorporated into the fairgrounds. The

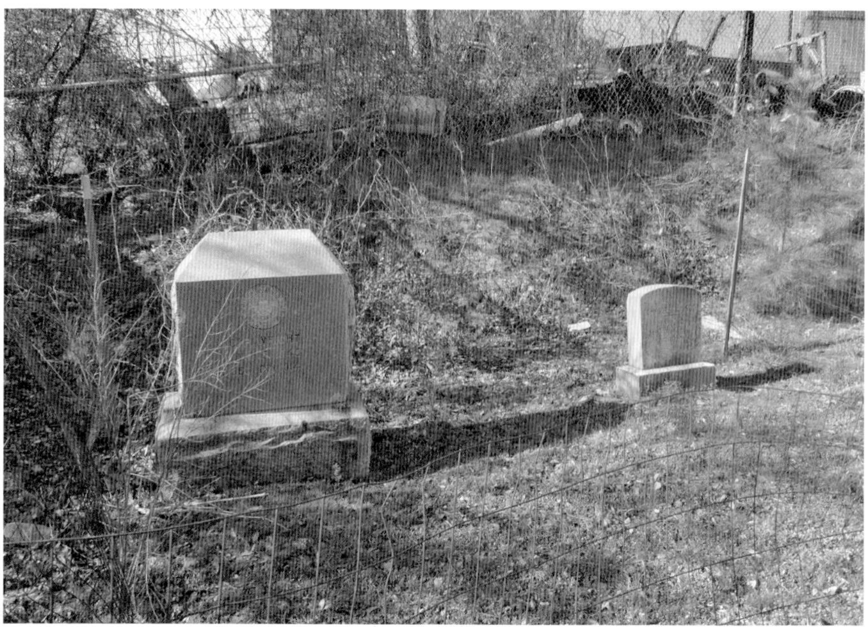

Graves at Fairgrounds Cemetery, Searcy, Arkansas.

two tombstones were moved up the hill near the country garage, but the bodies were never moved from their final resting places." What became of the other hundred or so graves? Were they moved to other cemeteries, or are they still at the fairgrounds, unmarked below the feet of thousands of happy unsuspecting fair-goers?

The following is from a news clipping from the *White County Record* of September 15, 1877:

> *Our County Poor House*
> *This institution is now under the supervision of W.S. Knox, Esq. and is situated one mile and a half from the Court House on what is known as Backbone Ridge, near the public road. The buildings are good, substantial box-houses—two of them, two rooms each. The rooms are not furnished with fine carpets and elegant furniture, neither are there any beautiful and costly pictures hung on the wall, but the floors looked neat and clean and the plain, common furniture, though in structure, are robed with neat and comfortable looking bedding, etc. The occupants, not withstanding, they look as though they were cared for in a comfortable and substantial way, are*

paupers, indeed, of which there are nine. They seem to be happy and their emaciated faces beam with delight on seeing the face of anyone whom they may meet, thus giving every evidence, though they be "poor in purse they are rich in soul." True, they seem to be a little chagrined on account of their misfortune and having to become inmates of a poor house, yet that sparkling glance of their eyes bespeaks for them an unbounded gratefulness that their fellow creatures have even supplied them with a home like this to dwell in while they are subjects of charity and dependent upon the world for support.

For the information of our readers and the tax payers in general we have visited the above house and spent an hour with paupers and found them as we have described them and for further edification we still give their, etc. Seth Dabbs and his two children are the first that we will notice. Mr. Dabbs is only a resident of the county for 2 years and came from Tennessee, he is afflicted with rheumatism. His wife is also there though she is not on the county. Next comes Sam Murray, an old gentleman about 55 years old and had been a resident of the county some 20 years. He is blind, or nearly so. Henry Evans, who is about 37 years old is another, he is down with the rheumatics and has been on the county for the last 6 or 7 years. These are all the men at the poor house.

The rest of the inmates are helpless women and children who are unable on account of feebleness to make support and have no one to look for help but from the county. In our conversation with them we found that they fared very well and wanted for nothing that was reasonable. They had plenty of good clothing and had sufficient variety of food so as to live even better than they did when they depended upon their own resources. In fact, we were agreeably surprised at finding the poor house so clean and the paupers doing so well.

It speaks volumes for our county and should be a source of great pleasure to all to know that they were doing something to support the poor and needy.

Little is known of the County Paupers' Farm except that it existed and that many people lived and died there. For many folks in the area, it seems that a few of the former residents may even linger there to this day, but in spirit only. People have reported seeing apparitions in the area, as well as hearing voices and being touched when no one is near. Could the ghostly phenomena experienced at the White County Fairgrounds be the result of the dead not being at rest due to the fact that their earthly remains lay trampled and unnoticed by the thousands of people who walk over them every year? I would have to say that if anything could cause a haunting, this would be it!

COUSINS CEMETERY, "MYSTERY GIRL'S GRAVE"

JUDSONIA

Cousins Cemetery, or the "Highway Roadside Mystery Grave," can be found in a fenced area in a triangle formed when the northbound lanes of Highway 67/167 and Highway 157 merge in Judsonia, Arkansas. The single grave site is enclosed by a fence and is shaded by a large tree that bears a figurine of an angel. A great many drivers have wondered, as they drive eastward, what the purpose of this oddity could be. It is the final resting place of an unknown child whose identity has conjured conflicting tales over the years. Some say the grave is that of a baby girl from a poverty-stricken family who died around 1890 when she overturned a high chair she was sitting in and landed on a knife. Others say a Native American princess is buried there. Whoever she truly is, the residents of Judsonia have adopted the child as one of their own and placed a tombstone on the grave that reads: "The Unknown Baby Girl; In Death She Belongs to All of Us." No one knows for sure who this child really was or what happened to her.

One version of the story claims that the grave is that of a baby girl, not quite two years old, who died in a high chair accident sometime around 1890. The child is said to have died of a knife wound, which she received when her high chair tipped over. In some manner, the baby had taken a large knife from the table near which her chair had been placed. Then, by shoving against the table, she managed to overturn the rickety chair that she sat in, and the knife plunged into her chest and she fell to the floor and died on the spot.

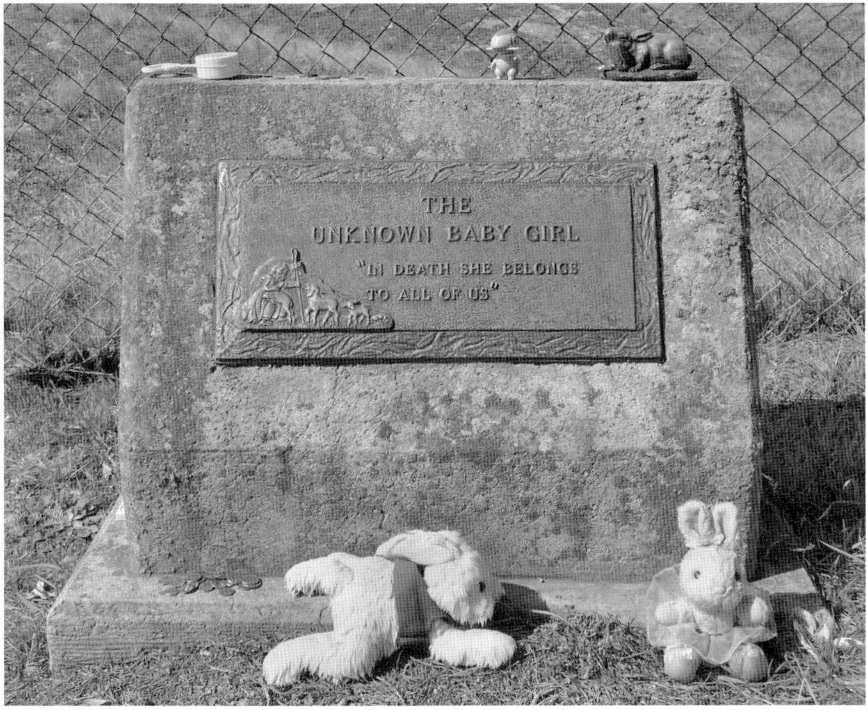

The Mystery Girl's Grave, Judsonia, Arkansas.

Her family were but poor tenants on the farm and could not afford to have their child buried in Evergreen Cemetery, which had been in use for approximately sixteen years at the time of her death. The owner of the farm at that time was a man by the name of Bunte. His land adjoined that of the Hopper farm. With the help of neighbors and friends, a crude casket was constructed and the baby's body was buried in a fence corner on the Bunte property. Many years later, adjustments were made to the property lines, and the grave was found to be within the Hopper property. Many locals believe that the baby's last name was Cousins.

Another account of the story tells of a party of American Indians who came through the area and left behind the remains of a little Indian girl who died there. Legend tells that one day a migrant party of American Indians came to the home of Dr. S.H. Burkhausen near Judsonia. Dr. Burkhausen was not at home when the party arrived, but they spoke to his daughter Martha. "We need a white man's doctor," they told Martha. "The little girl is very sick."

Martha placed her hand on the child's forehead. It was hot with a high fever. She then placed a towel soaked in cold water on the little girl's head and explained to the Indians that her father was not at home. "You do need a doctor," she told them. "Take her to Judsonia right now."

The Indians went on and camped on the outskirts of town. That night, the little Indian girl died. Either secretly or with permission, the Indians took the small body to a spot just outside the northern boundary of Evergreen Cemetery and buried it there. Local lore states that she was buried on the third day of July.

For years afterward, those who started down Judson Avenue to the Independence Day celebration grounds in the city park saw a stranger sight than anything they would ever see on the midway. The Indians would return year after year after the girl's death and perform their ancient ceremonies around the burial mound. What is not known is who she was and why she was so important that she warranted this sort of ritualistic ceremony on this particular day.

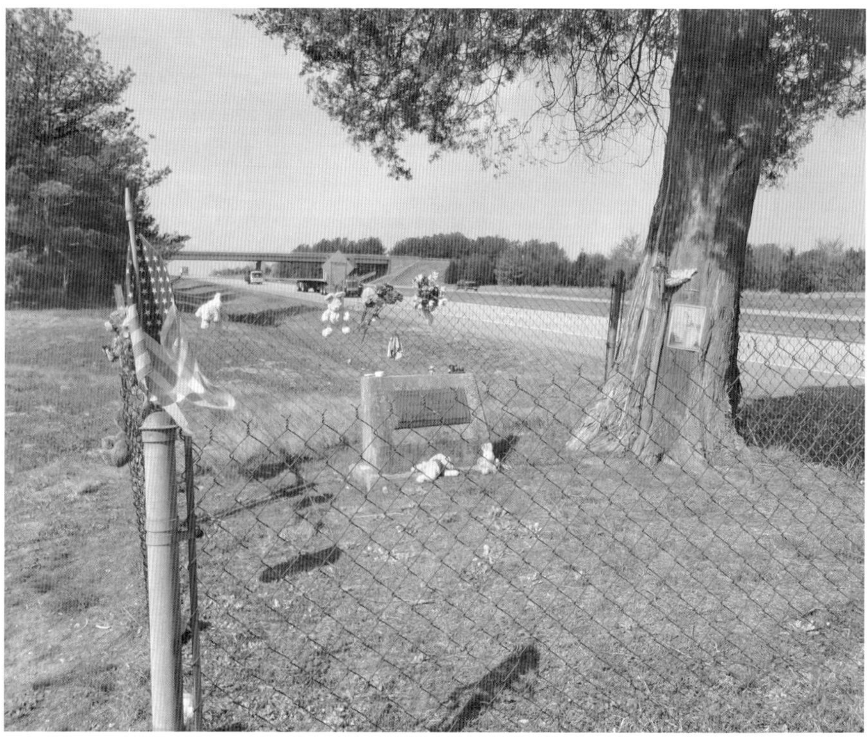

The Mystery Girl's Grave.

When surveys were being made for the new highway in 1965, local residents took the information about the grave site to Arkansas Highway Department officials. At that time, it seemed improbable that the new four-lane complex would follow the route to which it was eventually assigned. Later, the favored route surveys showed that near Bald Knob, the highway would have to pass through a large cemetery, which would present insurmountable problems. The engineers then chose the present route, and the small grave fell within the highway department's jurisdiction. The fence was erected, a tree was allowed to remain at the side of the mound and the small grave remains today.

Regardless of which story is true, hundreds of motorists pass the site every day, many even seeing the apparition of a small girl standing on the highway near the grave. Perhaps, as her story becomes known, the spirit of the "little mystery girl" can finally find some peace and Judsonia can help all America renew its dedication to the welfare of children everywhere. After all, she belongs to all of us now.

Shady Grove Cemetery

Bald Knob

Shady Grove Cemetery is located on the east side of Highway 67/167 approximately one mile south of the junction of U.S. Highways 64 and 67 at Bald Knob. The cemetery is divided into two sections, with the western section being much older. While both are well maintained, the western section is where the bulk of the ghostly occurrences have been reported over the years. It is said that when you enter the graveyard at night, you will be greeted with a burst of cold air, which many believe may be the presence of spirits coming up to greet you. Others say that if you enter in your vehicle at night and let your windows fog up, handprints will appear all over them, many being those of children. Others say that for the handprints to appear you must first flash your lights on and off three times. Crickets and grasshoppers are said to never enter the graveyard, even in the sweltering heat of the summer months. Many local folks have reported seeing apparitions of the dead wandering the cemetery at night, and some say that on a windless, cold night, if you listen very carefully you can hear the tormented souls of the dead begging to be released from Hell's dimension.

On my recent visit to Shady Grove Cemetery, I noticed nothing really out of the ordinary with the exception of one odd occurrence. Upon entering the old section of the cemetery, my companions and I noticed a very small puppy that sat near the grave of what we later discovered to be a small child who died early in the 1900s. As we approached the puppy, it became very aggressive toward us, growling and showing its teeth as to ward us off. We found this to be very odd, as the dog appeared to be only weeks old and not

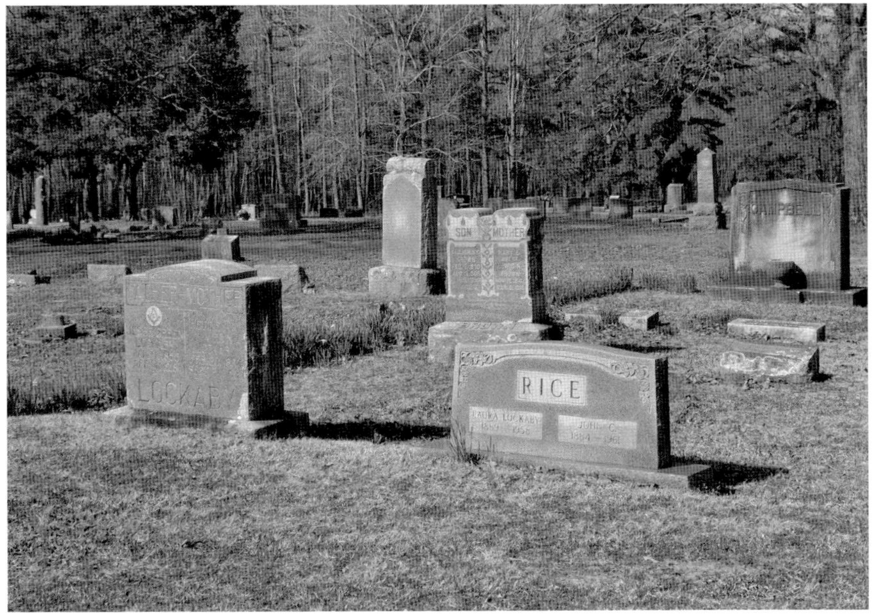

Shady Grove Cemetery, Bald Knob, Arkansas.

nearly old enough to be weaned from its mother. After agitating the puppy long enough, we decided to return to our vehicle and leave the cemetery. As we passed by the grave that the puppy was holding vigil on, we noticed that it had vanished. Could it be that what we had experienced was the apparition of a puppy that was standing vigil on its owner's grave? I guess we'll never know for sure, but I did find it very odd that three men could be so intimidated by such a small innocent creature.

Robinson Cemetery, "Red Eye Cemetery"

Jacksonport

Robinson Cemetery, known locally as "Red Eye Cemetery" for the red eyes visitors have reportedly spotted in this hilly cemetery that overlooks pasture lands and railroad tracks, is the final resting place for many of the more influential folks who founded Jacksonport and others who were among the more notable in its heyday during the Civil War. From a scientific standpoint, Robinson Cemetery has many of the triggers associated with paranormal activity. The cemetery is situated on a limestone bluff and sits above a river with railroad tracks running just next to it. Several of these elements are considered by paranormal researchers to be a perfect cocktail for paranormal activity due to them creating or retaining energy. These elements are believed to be key for spirits to manifest or make their presence known.

During the 1800s, the availability of transportation could determine the life and the death of many Arkansas towns. Jacksonport on the White River is a good example. It was created by the steamboat trade but declined when the railroad bypassed the town. In 1831, Thomas Todd Tunstall, steamboat captain and veteran of the War of 1812, piloted the little steamboat *Waverly* up the White River. It was the first steamboat to come up the river as far as Batesville. There was a deep, clear channel as far as the mouth of the Black River, above which the channel was obstructed with many gravel and sandbars. Two years later, Captain Tunstall bought a section and a quarter of land just below the mouth of the Black River. By 1839, the captain and his son William Tunstall had a plan drawn up for a town where a steamboat

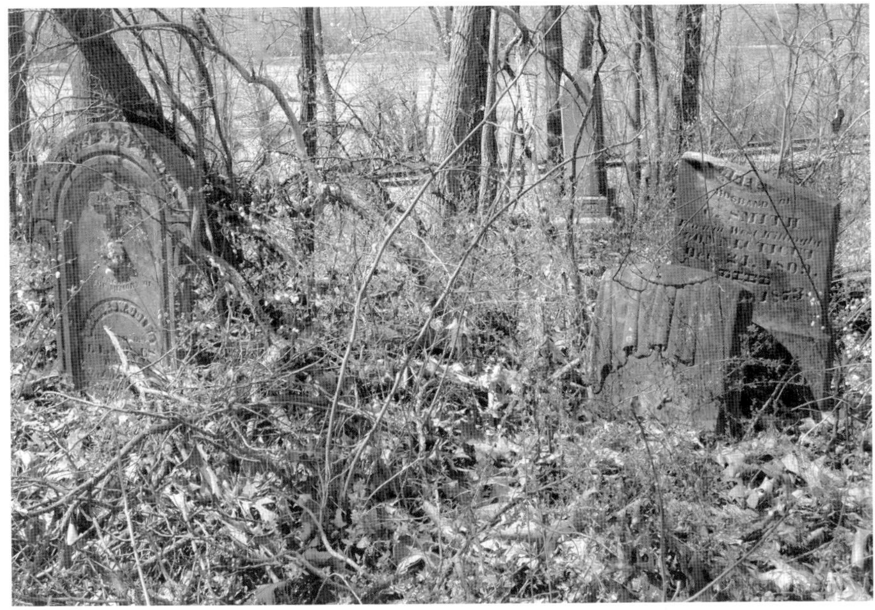

Graves at Robinson Cemetery, "Red Eye Cemetery," Jacksonport, Arkansas.

landing had been established. They named it Jacksonport in honor of President Andrew Jackson.

Thus began one of the most important towns in northeast Arkansas. Because of the deep and clear channel up the White River to this point, many steamboat owners made their headquarters and homes in Jacksonport. Wealthy landowners, lawyers, doctors and cotton buyers also came to Jacksonport in droves.

Steamboats carried timber from hardwood forests, cotton from the plantations and even wild game, bear grease and hides. These goods went to Memphis, New Orleans and many other destination markets in the South. On their return trips to Jacksonport, the boats brought fine furniture and all the luxuries of a growing community: coffee, spices, sugar, salt, medicine, molasses and even fine wines. Business trips, wedding trips and pleasure trips to other river ports kept the steamboats busy. Many boats lingered for four or five days, the captain enjoying the hospitality of the town. The steamboat bands played for local dances and for parties given by the captain on his boat. Pete Bach's Saloon or the Tunstall Tavern were the popular meeting places for the steamboat men and the planters who came to town to ship out their bales of cotton.

Throughout the Civil War, Jacksonport became a strategic objective for both sides, as the transport of supplies was heavily dependent on control of local rivers. In contrast to more pro-Union areas in the hills to the north, Jacksonport was overwhelmingly sympathetic to the secessionist cause, much to the repugnance of occupying Union soldiers. Permanent, secure control of Jacksonport was elusive for both Union and Confederate forces, even after the successful Union occupation of Little Rock (Pulaski County) in September 1863, as Rebel raiding campaigns harassed Federal forces in northern Arkansas until the end of the war. When the Union army invaded Arkansas during the Civil War, Jacksonport was occupied by Northern generals Frederick Steele and Samuel Curtis on May 3, 1862. Because of its importance as a river port, Jacksonport became the target for skirmishes by both the North and the South; whoever occupied Jacksonport could control north central Arkansas. The town and country were occupied by one army or the other during the entire four years of the war.

Jacksonport is also where Confederate general Jeff Thompson, "Swamp Fox of the Confederacy," formally surrendered the northern Arkansas army of more than five thousand to Union military authorities in 1865. Records indicate that Thompson made his farewell address to his troops from the deck of a steamboat. Could it have been the same steamboat belonging to Captain Albert Smith, who is buried at "Red Eye"?

According to historical accounts, Smith operated several boats in the area under the names of *Alberta and Winnie*, *Alberta 2* and *Alberta 3*, Alberta being the name of a favored daughter. He ran mostly on the upper White River and was involved primarily in trade. At Captain Smith's grave site, one of my fellow Ozarks Paranormal Society team members, Shane Wade Corkren, was taking photographs of the captain's tombstone, and as he stepped back to get a better shot, his left leg plunged through the ground right into the captain's grave. We were all quite shocked by this and soon recalled that we were warned by locals to watch where we stepped while up at Red Eye.

Upon entering the graveyard, we were quite shocked to see the state that it was in. There was evidence of it being used as a paintball course as well as a local party spot due to the trash and old liquor bottles that were scattered about. Many of the grave markers appeared to have been smashed. Most disheartening was evidence of it being used as an ATV course, with tire trails going everywhere and many of the tracks going right over of the tombstones. In the 1950s, a dirt road was cut directly through the cemetery, and now due to erosion many of the graves have been exposed to the elements and bones of the dead can be found lying about.

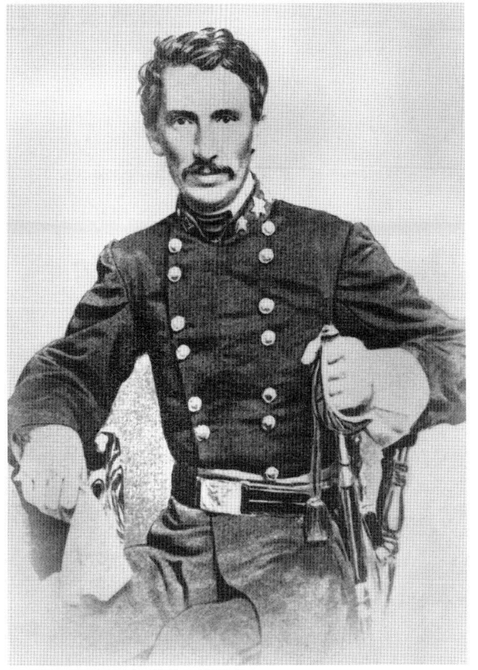

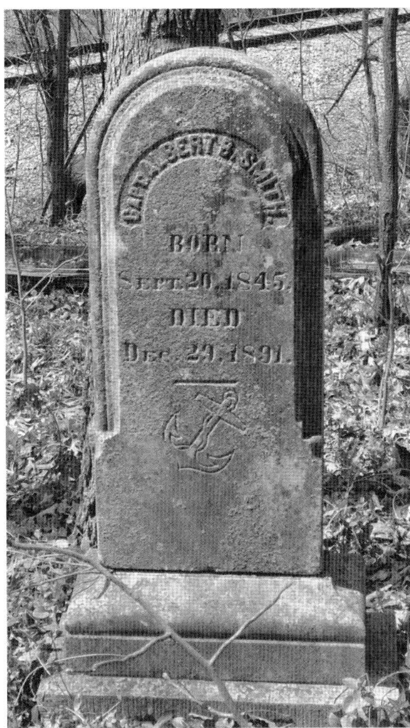

Above, left: Confederate General Jeff Thompson, "Swamp Fox of the Confederacy." *Courtesy of the Library of Congress.*

Above, right: The grave of Captain Albert Smith in Robinson Cemetery.

Many other influential people from the town's heyday are also buried at Red Eye, including the architect for the original Jacksonport courthouse; an Episcopal minister who built a church in town and performed lots of weddings for soldiers before they went off to fight in the Confederate war; and members of the Bach family, German immigrants. The Baches owned a saloon in town, and it seems that their children didn't fare so well, as many of the Bach children are buried at Red Eye, with most of them being infants and toddlers.

The largest monument in the cemetery is a white granite obelisk that is now toppled over. It marks the grave of the influential community leader Harrison Dwinal (1814–1868). Dwinal was a merchant who also served on the local vigilante committee during the Civil War. Locals used to call this the glowing graveyard because of his tombstone. Locals say it glows in the dark, but it's more likely that there is a lot of phosphorous in the stone. Other sightings in the cemetery have also been reported.

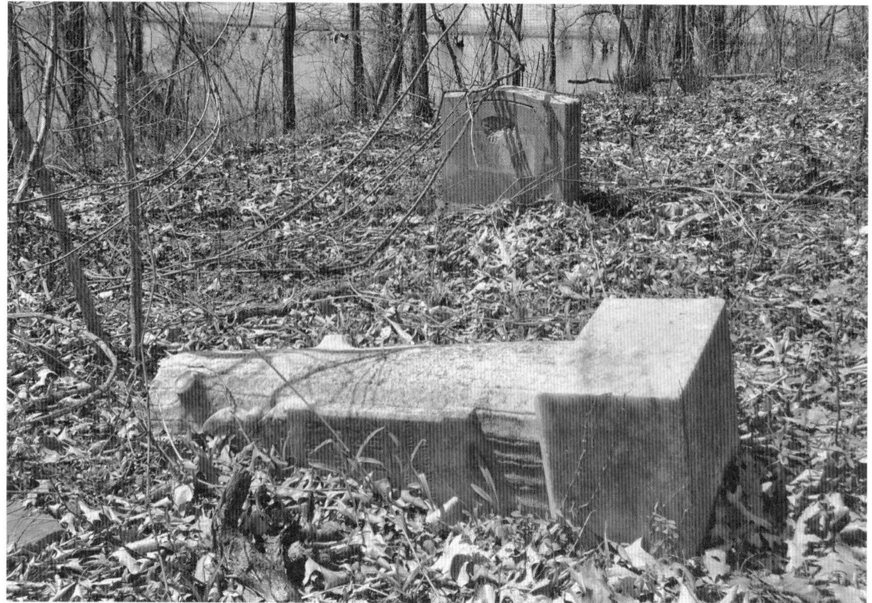

The grave of Harrison Dwinal in Robinson Cemetery.

Many have witnessed seeing a Confederate soldier with an old musket, and others have seen a girl sitting on a ridge near a tombstone. She looks to be wearing buckskin; locals call her the Indian girl. While at the cemetery, I experienced hearing a voice of a female whispering in my ear on several occasions. While it wasn't clear what the voice was saying, I knew it was not anyone with me that day due to the fact that I was accompanied by two other male team members.

As trade revived after the war, Jacksonport once again flourished. The new big steamboats *R.P. Walt*, *Legal Tender*, *Pat Cleburne*, *Hard Cash* and the *Milt Harry* made weekly trips to Jacksonport, all carrying up to two hundred passengers.

The future seemed assured. But just three miles east of Jacksonport, the Cairo and Fulton Railroad was laying its track. Railroad people had told Jacksonport officials that they would swerve west from the north–south line to include the town if the town would pay the railroad $25,000 for the additional cost of the track. Businessmen were insulted that Jacksonport was not automatically included on the main line, and they still had the river with all those big steamboats tying up at the landing every week. The offer was turned down.

That was the death knell for Jacksonport. By 1880, much of the trade had shifted to the faster means of transportation, and the town of Newport began to grow around the railroad loading station and the main line. Business and families followed, and in 1892, the county seat was moved to Newport, which also touched the White River. The big steamboats ceased to go up to Jacksonport, seven miles by river from Newport.

Today, the town of Jacksonport is merely a ghost of its proud past. Very few of the original structures remain. The most notable standing structure from Jacksonport's heyday is its majestic old courthouse. If you're brave enough to venture to Robinson Cemetery, stop in at the visitors' center at the Jacksonport State Park and ask for directions. Just getting to the old graveyard is an adventure in itself.

Auman Church and Cemetery

Harrison

Located north of Harrison, Arkansas, just off Highway 62 heading toward Alpena is the Auman Church and Cemetery. According to many local accounts, this place is a paranormal hotspot. Over the years, many people have captured EVPs (electronic voice phenomena) both in the old church as well as in the cemetery. One example captured the voice of a female child singing, and another recording captured the voice of a man screaming out, "I don't know what to do!" over and over again. Some folks report hearing the voices of children laughing and singing in the old church, and some have heard voices of children crying and even sneezing throughout the cemetery grounds. Others have captured what appear to be shadow people in photographs, and some have even captured this phenomenon on film. Now sitting vacant and no longer used as a place of worship, the well-kept church is a testament to the many souls that are laid to rest in the cemetery that surrounds it. Some of the graves go back as far as the mid-1800s, and many more recent burials are there as well.

The one thing that struck me most on my visit to this cemetery was the great number of small children who are buried here, most having died in the late 1800s, likely from one of the many pandemics that swept the area in those times. The feelings of sadness and loneliness were almost overwhelming in this cemetery as I wandered about reading the stones of the dead. After leaving the cemetery, the feelings seemed to linger with me for a few minutes but soon left.

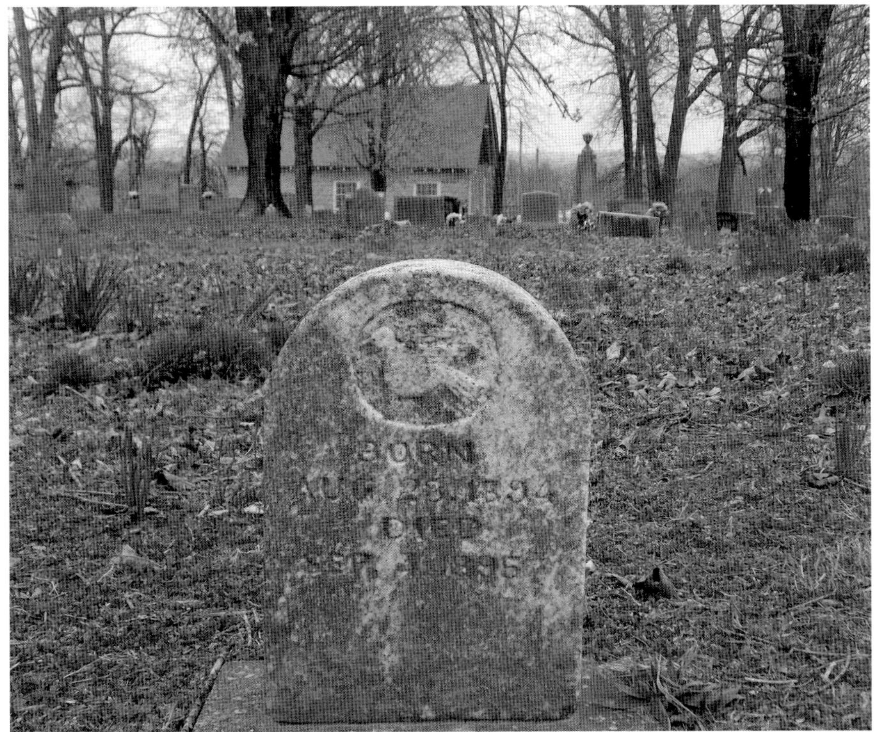

Auman Church and Cemetery, Harrison, Arkansas.

Other visitors to Auman have reported more ominous claims of paranormal activity. One couple states that late one moonlit night they arrived at the cemetery in hopes of capturing some EVPs, and as they entered the graveyard, something large and black without any real form rushed toward them, causing them to flee back to their truck and vacate the area in a sheer panic. They both felt that they were in real danger from something unknown. I'm not sure what's really going on at Auman Church and Cemetery, but I do plan on taking my paranormal team there one day soon to search for some answers to the paranormal activity that seems to plague it.

CONCLUSION

After many decades of research and investigation into the paranormal, I have come to the conclusion that many ghost stories can be explained without reference to anything paranormal. Many of these tales and experiences can be attributed to superstition, fear, history and environmental factors such as high electromagnetic fields (EMF). EMFs are known to mimic physical and mental symptoms often attributed to a haunting such as hallucinations, feelings of being watched, paranoia, headaches and varied host of pains in the body. Other naturally occurring factors may be at play as well. Tricks of the eye such as light and shadow could be the culprit as well. Combine all these elements with a self-fulfilling wish of actually believing or wanting to experience seeing or coming into contact with a ghost, and there you have it: the perfect recipe for a haunting.

With all these factors aside, there are things out there that can't be explained by debunking them as something occurring naturally as we perceive it—things that all the latest scientific equipment cannot debunk; things we are left with after all other avenues have been explored; things that may very well be paranormal in nature. Whether these experiences can truly be the spirits of the dead now long departed reaching out to us for some sort of resolution or attention, or something in the universe that science has not yet been able to interpret or explain, I cannot say. What I have learned is that the souls of many of the folks who once called the Ozarks home may very well linger on with us today. Whether they be a trick of the mind or something otherworldly, the belief that ghosts do exist is alive and well here in the Ozarks.

BIBLIOGRAPHY

Books and Articles

Campbell, William. *One Hundred Years of Fayetteville, 1828–1928*. Fayetteville, AR: self-published, 1928.

Crawford, Sybil F. *Jubilee: The First 150 Years of Mount Holly Cemetery, Little Rock, Arkansas*. Little Rock, AR: August House, 1993.

Crawford, Sybil F., and Mary F. Worthen. *Mount Holly Cemetery, Little Rock, Arkansas, Burial Index, 1843–1993*. Little Rock, AR: August House, 1993.

Goodspeed Publishing Company. *Goodspeed's Biographical and Historical Memoirs of Western Arkansas*. N.p., 1891.

Harman, S.W. *Hell on the Border: He Hanged Eighty-Eight Men*. 1898. Repr., Lincoln: University of Nebraska Press, 1992.

Harrington, Fred Harvey. *Hanging Judge*. 1951. Repr., Norman: University of Oklahoma Press, 1996.

Langford, Ella M. *History of Johnson County, Arkansas: The First Hundred Years*. N.p., 1921.

Mills, Letha, and H.K. Stewart. *Little Rock: A Contemporary Portrait*. Chatsworth, CA: Windson Publications, 1990.

Moshinskie, Jim. *Early Arkansas Undertakers and Embalmers*. Survey Book I. N.p., 1978.

Parler, Mary Celestia, ed. *Folk Beliefs from Arkansas: Death and Funereal Customs, Collected by University Students*. Vol. 8. Special Collections. Fayetteville: University of Arkansas Libraries, 1962.

Randolph, Vance. *Ozark Magic and Folklore*. New York: Dover Publications, Inc., 1964.

Reames, Clark. "History of Jacksonport." *Stream of History* 21 (September 1984): 18–22.

Richards, Ira Don. *Story of a Rivertown: Little Rock in the Nineteenth Century*. Benton, AR, 1969.

Shea, William L. "A Semi-Savage State: The Image of Arkansas in the Civil War." *Arkansas Historical Quarterly* 48 (Winter 1989): 320–23.

Thompson, George H. *Arkansas & Reconstruction*. Port Washington, NY: Kennikat Press, 1976.

Tuller, Roger H. *"Let No Guilty Man Escape": A Judicial Biography of "Hanging Judge" Isaac Parker*. Norman: University of Oklahoma Press, 2001.

Watson, Lady Elizabeth. *Fight and Survive! A History of Jackson County, Arkansas in the Civil War*. Conway, AR: River Road Press, 1974.

West, Mabel. "Jacksonport, Arkansas: Its Rise and Decline." *Arkansas Historical Quarterly* 9 (Winter 1950): 231–58.

Online Sources

The Encyclopedia of Arkansas History & Culture. www.encyclopediaofarkansas.net.

Forgotten USA. www.forgottenusa.com.

Ghosts & Haunts in Missouri. www.missourighosts.net.

National Cemetery Administration. "Fort Smith National Cemetery." www.cem.va.gov/CEM/cems/nchp/ftsmith.asp.

Orr, W.E. "Cousins Cemetery, Judsonia, Arkansas." www.argenweb.net/white/cems/Cousins_Cemetery_files/cousins_cemetery_judsonia.htm.

The Poorhouse Story. www.poorhousestory.com.

Popper, Joe. "Bertha Gifford: A Darkness 'Round the Bend." www.berthagifford.com.

The Shadowlands. www.theshadowlands.net.

Stewart, Charles W. "Fayetteville (Washington County)." Encyclopedia of Arkansas History and Culture. www.encyclopediaofarkansas.net/encyclopedia/entry-detail.aspx?search=1&entryID=1006.

Wikipedia. "Isaac Parker." www.en.wikipedia.org/wiki/Isaac_Parker.

About the Author

Originally from Fresno, California, David Harkins now resides in the Ozark Mountains of Missouri. In 1980, David helped launch an occult bookstore in Fresno that is still in operation today. During the early years at the bookstore, folks would come into the shop and share stories of their homes being haunted by things they believed to be of a paranormal nature. With a fascination with all things occult and paranormal, David began investigating these claims of supposed paranormal activity and soon got hooked on the fact that some of these claims may actually be occurring. After moving to the Ozark Mountains in 1985, David began investigating different locations in the Ozarks and eventually encountered others with the same interest in the paranormal.

In 2006, after meeting more folks in the area with a strong lure to the paranormal, David founded The Ozarks Paranormal Society (TOPS). Since forming TOPS, David has been featured on radio, print and television. Most notably, he and his team were featured on the Travel Channel program *Legends of the Ozarks* investigating the activity at Wilson's Creek National Battlefield near Springfield, Missouri. In 2013, The Ozarks Paranormal Society became official family members of the world-renowned paranormal team The Atlantic Paranormal Society (TAPS).

In April 2013, David and his fellow TOPS team member Bud Steed hosted the Ozarks Paracon, the first-ever paranormal conference of its kind in the Ozarks, at the Abou Ben Adhem Shrine Mosque in Springfield, Missouri. After the conference, they also led the first paranormal investigation ever allowed at the shrine.

Over the years, David has investigated many places in the United States, as well as Europe and India, and he continues his journey through the paranormal world to this day.

Visit us at
www.historypress.net

This title is also available as an e-book